science
short course

KU-452-929

The Open
University

S199 Weather and Climate Modelling

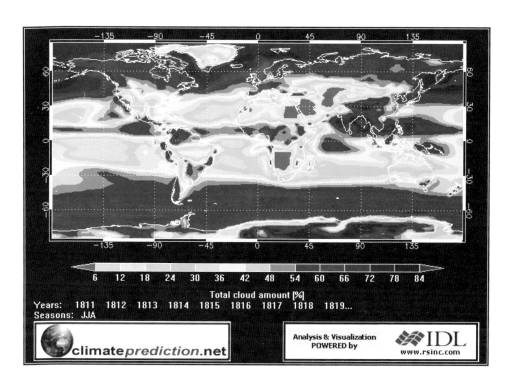

This publication forms part of an Open University course S199 Modelling the Climate. Details of this and other Open University courses can be obtained from the Student Registration and Enquiry Service, The Open University, PO Box 197, Milton Keynes, MK7 6BJ, United Kingdom: tel. +44 (0)870 333 4340, email general-enquiries@open.ac.uk

Alternatively, you may visit the Open University website at www.open.ac.uk where you can learn more about the wide range of courses and packs offered at all levels by The Open University.

To purchase a selection of Open University course materials visit www.ouw.co.uk, or contact Open University Worldwide, Michael Young Building, Walton Hall, Milton Keynes MK7 6AA, United Kingdom for a brochure: tel. +44 (0)1908 858785; fax +44 (0)1908 858787; email ouwenq@open.ac.uk

The Open University
Walton Hall, Milton Keynes
MK7 6AA

First published 2005

Edited, designed and typeset by The Open University.

Printed and bound in the United Kingdom by CPI, Glasgow.

ISBN 0 7492 1417 1

1.1

Contents

Contributors

The following people were involved in the production of this course.

Bob Spicer	*Author/Academic Editor*
Sylvia Knight	*Author/Academic Editor*
Sean Ryan	*Academic Editor*
Isla McTaggart	*Course Manager*
Jenny Hudson	*Course Secretary*
Liz Whitelegg	*Science Short Course Programme Director*
Elaine McPherson	*Course Manager*
Joy Wilson	*Course Manager*
Bob Allgrove	*Reader*
Claire Rothwell	*Reader*
Professor Ian James	*External Assessor, University of Reading*
Steve Best	*Graphic Artist*
Greg Black	*Interactive Media Developer*
Carl Gibbard	*Graphic Designer*
Rafael Hidalgo	*Media Project Manager*
Pam Owen	*Graphic Artist*
Amanda Smith	*Editor*

Much of the material in this book was edited material from the following courses, and the contributions of their course teams are gratefully acknowledged: S103 Discovering Science, S269 Earth and Life, S216 Environmental Science and U316 The Environmental Web.

This book was motivated in part by the work of the climate*prediction*.net project team, and many of the examples of climate modelling used to illustrate the science are from that project. The contribution of the project team is gratefully acknowledged.

Foreword

Climate is a condition of life. Only recently have we learned to distinguish climate and weather. Until now most climatic variations have been slow and, between generations, scarcely perceptible. The mechanisms of climate have been even more mysterious than those of the weather. In the last forty years things have changed. With greater knowledge has come the uncomfortable realisation that climate change is, in the words of the [UK] Prime Minister, Tony Blair, the most important long-term issue we face as a global community: worse indeed, according to the Government's Chief Scientific Adviser, than the threat of terrorism.

At present the human foot is on the accelerator. But we cannot see exactly where we are going. The Earth system of which climate is part is immensely complex and sensitive to small perturbations. It is also non-linear. We know from the Intergovernmental Panel on Climate Change that most of the observed warming over the last fifty years is likely to have been due to the human-induced increase in greenhouse gas concentrations. These are steadily increasing as we move ever further from the norms of the last 750 000 years.

We need to know, and are far from knowing, what is likely to happen next. The questions are becoming clearer, but the answers are still elusive. This project explains the background, sets out the uncertainties, puts together the possibilities, tries out different models, and brings home in vivid fashion the intellectual fascinations as well as the frustrations of plotting the future. I wish those who follow the course all success.

Sir Crispin Tickell
UK Government Adviser on the Enviroment

Preface

This book introduces climate modelling. It looks at the scientific topics that underpin our understanding of the climate and at the scientific processes by which the climate is modelled. However, it is a little different from an ordinary book. Most people find that to get to grips with learning about a new subject it is helpful not just to read about it but to engage more actively with the text. So this book has questions scattered throughout it, which you are encouraged to try answering for yourself before looking at the answers that follow them. If you use this tool for learning you will find that it helps your understanding.

If you want to engage even more with the topic of this book, you could participate in a global experiment to model climate change. Many of the examples used in this book to illustrate climate modelling are from the climate*prediction*.net experiment. To download climate*prediction*.net on to your computer and run your own unique climate model, log on to the website at www.climateprediction.net, which includes a range of supplementary information, and news items about the project.

1 Introduction

'Climate is what you expect; weather is what you get.'
Edward Lorenz

Everyone takes an interest in weather. For some people it merely determines how to dress as they go about their daily lives. For others, such as farmers, it determines livelihoods, and for some people such as pilots and seafarers, it can literally determine life or death. Throughout human history the constant changes in the weather have been a topic of keen interest. However, until very recently, the climate – i.e. the weather we can expect in a certain place at a certain time – was assumed not to change much. As we have learned more about the past, it has also become clear that climate does indeed change, but over time-scales that are usually long compared with the average human lifespan. Occasionally, though, geological, and even archaeological, evidence suggests that sometimes significant changes in climate have occurred quickly, within decades. In this book we introduce the science of both weather (meteorology) and climate, we look at why neither are ever constant, and we shall explore together the latest tools that have been developed to understand and predict future changes.

Science is all about trying to understand how the Universe, including the Earth and everything related to it, works. Early scientists observed and described phenomena using words and diagrams and then, as science progressed, these qualitative observations were supplemented with numerical measurements. To aid our understanding of how something works we can build models. In general terms, a model is a way of representing a system, often on a smaller scale, for the purposes of reproducing, simplifying, analysing or understanding it.

A numerical model of something like the Earth's atmosphere combines data from observations of the atmosphere with equations which describe how various atmospheric properties, such as temperature and water content, relate to each other and how they are likely to change. By trying to describe the atmosphere in such mathematical terms, and letting this model run over many simulated years, we can investigate how the atmosphere might change with time, possibly in response to a hypothetical change, for example in its composition. Knowing what the future holds for us in terms of climate change is a pressing issue, and the quality of life for many millions of people, and even the continuance of their lives, depends on such predictions.

This book provides the background science to climate modelling. It progressively introduces the processes of energy absorption and transfer that drive the weather systems, together with basic concepts such as the composition of the atmosphere and the reactions that take place within it. By understanding what happens at the atomic and the molecular levels, science can explain the larger-scale phenomena that are familiar to us, such as the weather and, through that, climate and climate change.

The daily changes in weather at any one point on the Earth's surface are only one small part of the global meteorological system. Until now this larger picture was inaccessible to anyone making local weather observations because their view of the world was limited to what they could see as far as the horizon. With the virtual world created by a computer model, you can observe meteorological phenomena and processes anywhere in the world, on land or over the ocean, at ground level or high up in the atmosphere. Moreover, because hours in the real world are reduced to minutes in a model world, you can see how weather transforms into climate.

1.1 Weather and climate

Climate was defined above as 'the weather we can expect in a certain place at a certain time'.

● What are the main features of weather?

◌ The most obvious features are temperature, rainfall (or other forms of precipitation, such as hail or snow) and wind. These in turn are affected by features such as the amount of sunshine and cloud cover.

● Can you think of another way of expressing the difference between the terms 'weather' and 'climate'?

◌ 'Weather' means the day-to-day meteorological conditions at a particular place. 'Climate' means the long-term, prevalent weather conditions.

● The organisers of a sports event want to take out insurance against it raining on the day. Would each of the following groups be concerned with weather or climate: (i) the organisers; (ii) the statisticians who calculate the insurance premium; (iii) the insurance company's claims department; (iv) the visitors?

◌ (i) The weather: the organisers are interested in what happens on the day, but they may have a sense of unease based on their experience of the climate – what the weather is likely to be.

(ii) The climate: they need to know the probability of having to pay out compensation.

(iii) The weather: they are only interested in whether it rains on the day.

(iv) The weather: like the organisers, their experience of climate may help them decide whether to take an umbrella.

You may have concluded that it is not always easy to unravel weather and climate in a given set of circumstances.

Weather – that perennial topic of conversation – is an integral part of our daily lives. It influences what we wear, what items are stocked by shops, and our leisure activities. It can also cause serious damage (Figure 1.1) and even kill. We know from experience that weather is very variable. In parts of the world where the weather varies considerably from day to day, such as the UK, knowing what the weather is likely to be a few days ahead has economic and social implications, e.g. for harvesting crops or for the sports event you considered above. Although we know from experience that the weather can change from minute to minute, hour to hour and day by day, we are also aware that there are patterns in the weather. In northern Europe the summer tends to be warmer and drier than the winter, but in general cool temperatures predominate for much of the year and the air tends to be damp even when it is not raining. By contrast,

Figure 1.1 Weather can be very destructive. Not surprisingly, insurance companies are interested in the detail of future possible climate change.

in the Mediterranean region or California, for example, seasonal and daily weather variations are much less extreme and sunny days with clear skies are a feature of much of the year.

● For the same amount of compensation, do you think the premium for insuring against rain on the day of a sports event is likely to be higher or lower in California than it is in the UK?

◉ Other things being equal, it is likely to be lower. Rain is less common (climate) and there are fewer daily variations (weather), so the underwriters can be more certain of a rain-free outcome.

These general observations on the variability and different characteristics of weather suggest that there are patterns to weather – both over time in one location and spatially, from place to place, over the surface of the Earth. Figure 1.2 shows how three climate variables vary over the year in London. You might use similar graphs when choosing, for example, a holiday destination for a particular time of the year.

Figure 1.2 Average monthly climate data for London, based on more than 30 years of observations: (a) daily maximum (red) and minimum (blue) temperature in degrees Celsius (°C); (b) rainfall in millimetres (mm); and (c) hours of sunshine per day (h day^{-1}).

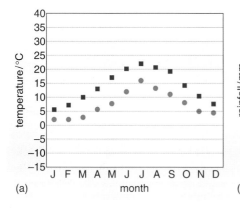

(a)

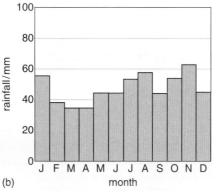

(b)

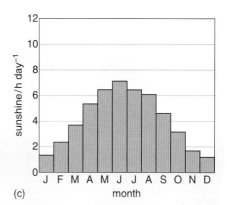

(c)

● Do you think the insurance premium against rain falling on the day of a sports event to be held in London would be greater for a February event than for one in July?

⬤ You may have found it somewhat harder to resolve this question. Figure 1.2b does not show great variations in rainfall over the year, but it does indicate that February is, on average, drier than July. So this suggests a lower February premium. However, Figure 1.2 does not tell you that small amounts of rain, say 0.25 mm, falling in a day is a more frequent event in February than in July, so the premium against rain falling on the day of the sports event should be lower in July. Even though less rain falls on average in February, there are typically more rainy (drizzly) days. The message here is that before using an 'average' value it is important to make sure we know what is meant.

We shall return to the use of 'average' or 'mean' values to show changes over time in Chapter 2.

In order to see spatial patterns, we use maps to show the distribution of, for example, average annual precipitation, as in Figure 1.3.

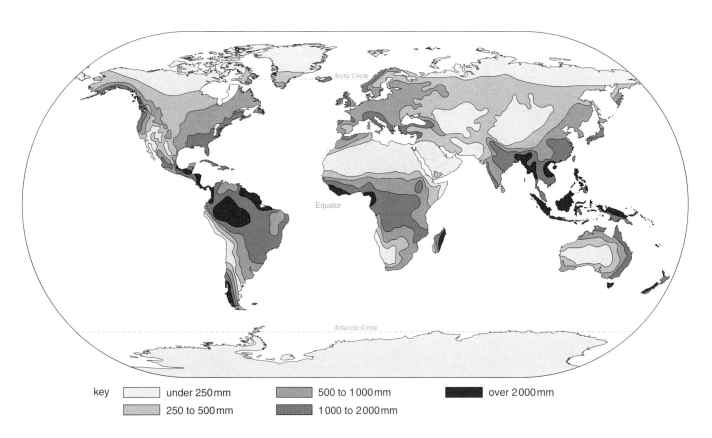

key ▢ under 250 mm   ▨ 500 to 1000 mm   ▨ over 2000 mm
    ▨ 250 to 500 mm   ▨ 1000 to 2000 mm

Figure 1.3 Map showing mean annual precipitation (rainfall, snow, etc.) around the globe. Different levels of annual precipitation in millimetres (mm) are represented by different shades, as given in the key.

- Describe the general patterns in global precipitation that you can see in Figure 1.3, in particular the regions of lowest and highest annual precipitation.

  The regions with similar levels of precipitation tend to form in bands parallel to the Equator. Regions with annual precipitation over 2000 mm generally occur fairly close to the Equator, such as South-East Asia, West Africa and Central and northern South America. Desert regions with under 250 mm precipitation a year occur slightly further away from the Equator, such as the Sahara, Arabian peninsula and Central Australia, and in the polar regions.

- What are these precipitation patterns most likely to relate to?

  The patterns are likely to relate to climate features, such as temperature and amount of water in the atmosphere (humidity), although they could also relate to topography, such as mountainous areas. The effect of the Andes in South America is particularly obvious in Figure 1.3.

Despite the day-to-day variability in weather, over time the same type of weather repeatedly occurs in any given location, so there is a high probability that the daily weather will be of a particular type. To illustrate this, think of the weather in London (see Figure 1.2). In any given week there is a high probability of rain, even in the summer months. By contrast, in the Sahara Desert rain is rare and it may not rain for many years at a time.

Climate differences result in different types of vegetation from place to place, as shown in Figure 1.4.

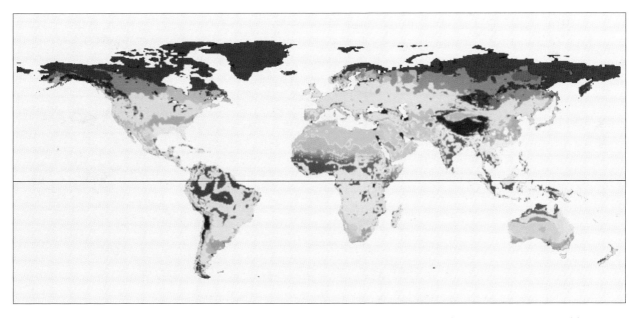

Figure 1.4 Map of global vegetation showing patterns of different vegetation types, represented by different colours. Here vegetation is classified on its overall appearance. So, for example, tundra, which consists of low-growing bushes and grasses, is dark blue, while the dense layers of trees and bushes of the tropical rainforests are red.

● How do the patterns in Figure 1.4 compare with those in Figure 1.3?

◑ Like precipitation, the vegetation patterns also tend to form in bands parallel to the Equator. As you would expect, tropical rainforest occurs in the areas of highest precipitation, while tundra occurs in the areas of lowest precipitation (although its distribution also relates to temperature and the duration of snow cover).

Plants that are not adapted to drought cannot survive in desert conditions. The plants that flourish in the tropics could not tolerate freezing conditions so would not live through a winter in a location where frost is a certainty on many nights. Repeated weather patterns in a particular place eliminate all those plants that are not suitably equipped to survive, leaving those that are. If there was no pattern to weather over long periods of time this process of selection and adaptation could not have happened.

These repeated weather patterns are what we know as 'climate'. In some senses climate can be thought of as 'average' weather. What we mean by 'average' here encompasses not only the kind of weather we are likely to experience at any given location but also the extent to which weather might be expected to vary from day to day, and even over several years. Climate, then, is a description of the particular type of weather that is expected to occur with high probability.

There is no clear definition of climate because how we assess what is the 'average' or 'normal' varies depending on what we are interested in. The climate information we need before deciding where to go for a holiday is quite different from what we might use if we are interested in explaining vegetation differences or global climate change. In the case of a holiday destination, we want to know how likely particular weather is at a particular resort at a particular time of year. When studying global vegetation or climate change, we might be interested in many places over longer time-scales.

This concept of 'average' or 'normal' is important in meteorology, where some idea of 'average' weather at a place can be documented by accumulating weather readings over many years (30 years is often used, as in Figure 1.2). Calculating averages even in this instance is not straightforward, as we shall see in Chapter 2, but the variations in the form and composition of vegetation demonstrate very clearly that geographic differences in average weather exist not only over a few decades (represented by the 30-year averages) but also over the centuries needed for forests to grow.

1.2 Historical records of climate

If the term 'climate' encompasses the concept of variation in weather, and global vegetation patterns show some constancy in climate patterns over centuries, what do we mean when we say the climate is changing? In particular, what do we mean by 'global warming'? To begin answering these questions we need to look at evidence of the climate over time-scales that are much longer than decades or centuries: that is, over geological time-scales. An understanding of past variations should help us to predict future variations, including those in the very near future.

Figure 1.5 shows the record of the Earth's global mean (average) surface temperature (GMST) over the last 1000 million years of the Earth's history. Note that there are no values for the temperature, so the graph is qualitative rather than quantitative. It illustrates variations in warmth or coolness relative to the present GMST. This style of graph is often used for displaying such data. Present day (i.e. time = 0) is at the top of the time-scale and moving lower down the scale means going further back in time. The solid red line represents the record of the Earth's GMST interpreted from fossils and other evidence preserved in rocks. The vertical dashed line represents today's GMST, so the solid line moves to the right of it when the temperature was higher than at present and to the left when the temperature was lower.

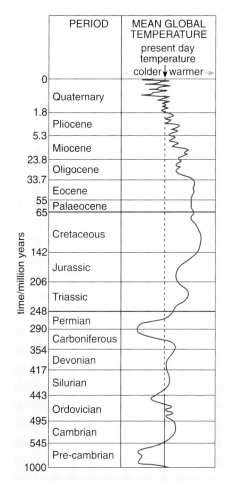

Figure 1.5 Variation in the Earth's global mean surface temperature (GMST) over the last 1000 million years, relative to the present value of +15 °C. Humans first appear in the Pliocene. 'Period' means the name given to the different segments of geological time.

- Examine the values on the time-scale, which are in millions of years. What do you notice about the spacing of these values and the smoothness of the fluctuations?

- Equal divisions on the time axis do not represent equal amounts of time, i.e. the time-scale is non-linear. It is more 'compressed' the further back in time we go and the record is much smoother. This time-scale allows us to see more detail of recent fluctuations in the GMST. Because the information we get from rocks and fossils is often less complete the further back in time we go, it follows that the amount of fine detail we can show diminishes.

The important point here is not the detail but, rather, that the line on the graph is rather wiggly. This means that, as far as we can tell from a variety of geological evidence, particularly fossils, the GMST and therefore the climate has never been constant. Variations occurred even before humans existed. It is a natural feature of climate that it varies over time, with or without human influence.

- Why does the line appear to wiggle more intensely as it approaches the present day?

- Some may be true fluctuations in temperature, but most of the *apparent* extra variation is caused by the more expanded time-scale in this part of the graph, so the variations are more clearly displayed. The briefer time-scale fluctuations in earlier periods are smoothed out by the compressed scale.

- Are there any time intervals during which the GMST may have been more or less constant? How reliable is your answer?

- Fewer variations in temperature appear between about 34 and 65 million years ago. However, there could have been large temporary fluctuations that are lost by the smoothing effect of the compressed time-scale. Note also that there are three intervals where temperatures were much colder than the present GMST, such as about 270 to 320 million years ago.

The GMST has changed measurably over the last few thousand years, but by much less than the fluctuations shown in Figure 1.5. Overall, the climate since the start of human civilisation has been much more stable than in any comparable-length period in the previous half-million years (as far back as this kind of 'high resolution' climate data extend). This may not be a coincidence: it would hard for agriculture to develop if climatic conditions keep changing. Over the past 10 000 years (the period of time known as the Holocene), vegetation patterns show that the rate of climate change has been slow compared with the time it takes for plants to migrate by seed dispersal and for forests to grow. This is why climate appears to be stable from the perception of a human lifetime. Although the rate of change has been historically slow, archaeological evidence clearly shows that climate change has, to a large extent, shaped human history and that sometimes, and in some places, the changes can be remarkably sudden.

In recent decades it has become apparent that a range of human activities, among other factors, have changed the composition of the atmosphere and that these changes alter the way in which energy is absorbed and transferred within the atmosphere. In turn, these changes may affect the most fundamental of climatic features – the temperature. Determining the rate of climate change, how it changes and what the pattern of change might be is the main reason so much effort has gone into developing climate models.

1.3 Recent global climate change: the expert view

This section gives a brief picture of the current scientific consensus on global climate change.

The Intergovernmental Panel on Climate Change (the IPCC) is an international organisation made up of thousands of scientists, from a range of disciplines, whose role is to review all the available scientific evidence about the risk of 'human-induced climate change'. Their 2600-page report in 2001 concluded that there is clear evidence for a 0.6 °C rise in the GMST during the 20th century. Figure 1.6 shows the compilation of temperature data illustrating fluctuations that have occurred in the GMST since 1860. Note that the temperature in individual years is uncertain. This uncertainty is shown by plotting a short vertical line, rather than just a point, and using the length of the line to indicate the range of possible values for the temperature. Such lines are called error bars. It is apparent from the size of these bars that the uncertainties are larger the further back in time we go, but the more recent years are clearly warmer than the earlier years even allowing for this uncertainty. Despite the uncertainty in the GMST in any individual year, it was the consensus of the 122 main authors, and the 450 other scientists who reviewed the IPCC report, that global warming is happening. We shall look at uncertainties more in Chapter 2.

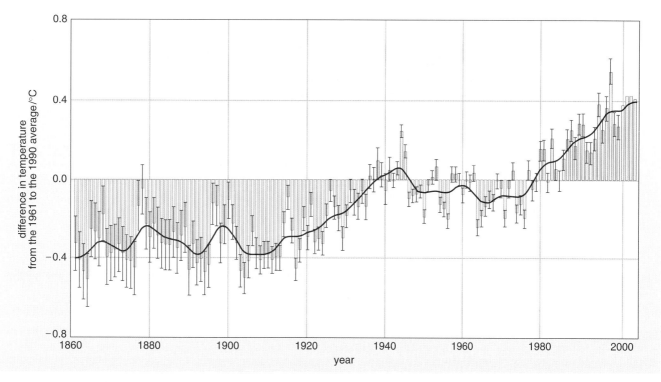

Figure 1.6 The difference in annual GMST from the 1961 to 1990 average (15.08 °C) between 1860 and 2003. (Data for 2000 to 2003 have been added to those published in the IPCC's 2001 report.) Note the error bars, which indicate the uncertainty in the measurements. Note also that the uncertainties are mostly smaller than the observed differences from the mean, indicating that the differences are real and not caused by measurement errors. The wavy solid line is a smoothed version of the data, which emphasises longer-term averages over the year-to-year variation.

The IPCC report also documents a 200 mm rise in global average sea-level over the last 100 years and a 40% reduction in the sea-ice thickness over the Arctic Ocean, a 40% increase in storm activity over the North Atlantic Ocean over the last 50 years, and mountain glaciers melting at the fastest rate ever recorded.

During 2002/3 the world saw a year of more extreme weather phenomena than ever before recorded and in 2004 there was some of the most intense hurricane activity so far observed. In England alone, 2000/2001 was the wettest on record with two 'once in 30 years' floods in the same month, while 2003 was one of the driest years on record. These wild fluctuations are characteristic of a climate system in a process of rapid change.

However, note that our methods of recording weather have also become more sophisticated, so there are hidden pitfalls in comparing recent and historical records. It is possible that there were similar events in the past but records have not survived. Nevertheless, there is considerable evidence that we are witnessing global change of a kind and at a rate that humans have never experienced.

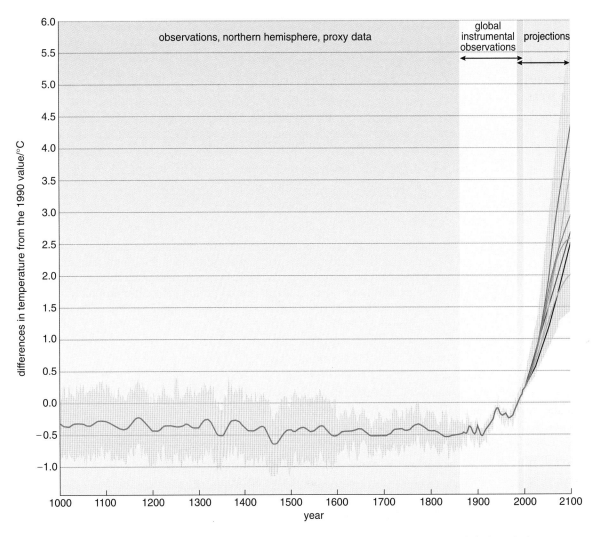

Figure 1.7 The predicted rise in GMST according to an array of different climate models in relation to the past record of observations (red line). Observations are made either indirectly (proxy data) or with instruments. The uncertainty is indicated by the grey zone. Each coloured line in the area marked 'projections' represents the warming as predicted by a different set of model conditions.

Under these circumstances it seems sensible to try to predict what will happen next. Even if we cannot stop climate change, it is as well to know what to expect and to plan accordingly. In this context the IPCC predicts that there could be a global rise in the GMST of as much as 5.8 °C by 2100 (Figure 1.7). Do not worry about the details of the graph, just note the general pattern of a very steep predicted rise in temperature, particularly in relation to the temperatures experienced before 1900. A warming of this magnitude would be substantially larger than anything that has occurred since human civilisation began.

Such global mean temperatures have not been experienced on our planet since Cretaceous times, 65 million years ago. There are, as we shall see, huge uncertainties in the IPCC prediction that limits its use for detailed planning. What we need to do is reduce the size of the uncertainties in the predictions. The climate*prediction*.net experiment, introduced in the preface to this book, is part of the ongoing effort to do just that. Results from the climate*prediction*.net experiment will make up part of the next IPCC report.

1.4   An introduction to weather and climate models

We noted at the start that a numerical model describes the attributes of a system and the processes at work in it. We now go on to see what this might mean for a model of the weather and/or climate. When we say we want to know what the weather is going to be, we tend to be interested in only a few of its attributes.

● What attributes of the weather are you commonly interested in?

▫ You might want to know how warm or cold it is going to feel (temperature), whether it is going to rain (the amount of water in the atmosphere and whether that water is going to fall to the ground), whether it will be windy (the speed at which the air moves), and so on.

Temperature, precipitation, wind speed and many other attributes of the weather can be measured. The values of the measurements of all the attributes together can be used to describe the weather numerically. It should not be a surprise, then, that we can also describe weather processes (the things that make the weather), and the way in which they interact, using numbers.

A very simple numerical model of weather might consider the heating effect of the Sun on a patch of ground. If we measure the amount of the Sun's energy arriving over an area of soil measuring 1 metre by 1 metre, and we know something about how much of the energy is absorbed and how much is reflected back into space, we can construct a simple mathematical model that describes how hot that patch of ground will become after a given amount of energy has arrived. Knowing something about how much heat is transferred from that patch of ground to the air above it will tell us how much the air will heat up, and so on. Now, instead of using a 1 m × 1 m patch of soil, we could do the same for the whole Earth. Knowing how much energy from the Sun falls on the Earth's surface and how much is absorbed, we can calculate how quickly the Earth will heat up. As it gets hotter it tends to lose more heat to space (it radiates heat – more of this in Chapter 3), so a time will come when the amount of heat received will balance the amount lost and the temperature will no longer rise. Such a simple model is called an energy balance model.

In Chapters 2 to 7 we examine several features of the Earth and the processes that affect its climate. A numerical model of the climate must be simpler than the actual climate. How much simpler depends on the type of model and what it is being used to understand: the more complex the model, the harder it is to relate a change in one factor to an effect on another. Furthermore, by attempting to simplify the climate, we introduce a degree of uncertainty.

The number of equations in the model and the values given to their individual parts mean there will probably be many factors that we are not certain about. We can construct many models using a range of acceptable values, but it is not easy to choose the best model. An important aspect of numerical modelling is trying to understand more about the inherent uncertainties.

In Chapter 8 we shall look at models that take into account all the different aspects of the climate system – not just the balance between the amount of heat received and the amount of heat lost. Such models also have to take into account all the interactions between the different elements of the climate system: for example, how the amount of cloud in the sky affects the temperature of the land surface (it feels cooler if a cloud passes overhead on an otherwise sunny day). For models to be created which can do this, we first have to understand how weather, and therefore climate, works. By Chapter 8, we shall see how the best climate models – called general circulation models – use all of this science to help us understand and predict the weather and, ultimately, the climate.

1.5 Summary of Chapter 1

1 Climate is the average, or mean, weather: in other words, the weather that experience has led us to expect. Therefore, we need to understand how the weather works before we can understand and predict the climate.

2 The climate varies with both location and time – the Earth's climate has always been changing.

3 In the last few decades the climate has been changing faster than humans have ever experienced before.

4 Climate models are used to understand the climate and to predict how it might develop in the future.

2 Surface temperature

In this chapter we shall explore one of the main features of weather and climate – temperature. We begin by asking the question, 'What is temperature?' As you will soon see, the short answer is 'energy'. We shall consider where the energy that drives the weather and climate comes from and goes to in Chapters 3 and 4. In this chapter, however, we shall see how the global mean surface temperature can be used to characterise the global climate and hence be used as a measure of climate change.

2.1 What is temperature?

An important feature of the weather and the climate is temperature. You will already be familiar with temperature from the sensations of warmth and coldness, but what is temperature from a scientific perspective? The temperature of a substance (air, water, soil, etc.) indicates the amount of random motion of its constituent atoms or molecules. You will learn more about the atomic and molecular nature of matter in Chapter 7; for now it is enough to know that the particles of matter are constantly jostling about and the more they jostle, the hotter the substance is. It takes energy (see Box 2.1) to make particles move, so the temperature of a substance is also a measure of how much energy of motion – so-called kinetic energy – its particles have. A high temperature corresponds to a high rate of internal motion and high kinetic energy of the substance's particles.

Figure 2.1 shows the variation of temperature at the Earth's surface over a 24-hour period in November, as worked out by a climate model in which the average temperatures are calculated every 30 minutes of model time. The solid line, which is the GMST, looks remarkably flat, which suggests that the average temperature of the whole of the Earth's surface varied by no more than a degree or so.

'The mathematical problem is not yet defined: there are more unknowns than equations.'
C.G. Rossby

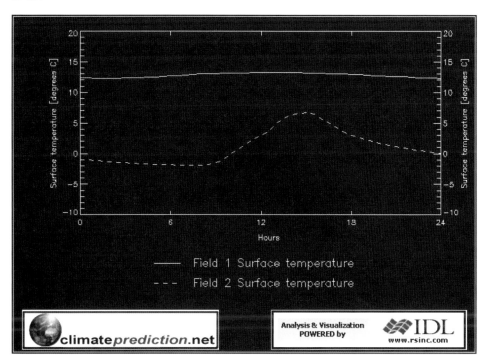

Figure 2.1 The global average surface temperature (solid line) over 24 hours in November compared with the average surface temperature in London (dashed line) (from a climate model).

Box 2.1   Energy

Energy is one of those words in common use but with a variety of everyday meanings, encapsulated in such phrases as 'I'm full of energy today'. 'Energy' also has a precise scientific meaning; indeed, it is one of the most important concepts in the whole of science.

● Think of two or three phrases in which you include the word 'energy' in an *everyday* sense.

◍ Some possible examples are: 'Where do those children get their energy from?'; 'I haven't got the energy to get up'; 'Sweets are full of energy'.

None of the everyday uses of the word 'energy' is very precise but they all encapsulate the notion that energy enables activity to take place. This is also at the heart of the scientific notion of energy. Energy is a physical property possessed by an object, and it is a measure of the object's capability to 'make things happen'. In order for things to happen, some of the energy in the object must be transferred to another object.

A common consequence of transferring energy to an object is to cause its temperature to rise. When we burn fuel under a pan of water, energy is transferred from the flame to the water and, as a result, the temperature of the water increases. Similarly, when an electric kettle is used to heat water, energy is transferred to the heating element from the electric current running through it and then energy is transferred from the element to the water.

Energy is a physical property of an object, so it can be measured and it has a unit of measurement. Although there are very many forms of energy, they can all be measured in the same unit. The internationally agreed unit of energy is the joule, which has the symbol J. Over the years, scientists and others have suggested several different units for measuring energy, including two others you might have heard of: the erg and the kilowatt-hour. Erg comes from the same Greek word as 'ergonomics', being associated with work or activity, while the kilowatt-hour is a favourite in the electricity industry. In an effort to standardise usage, not just for energy but for many other physical quantities as well, the Système International (SI) specifies which units should be used internationally. The joule is the agreed SI unit for energy.

The precise definition of the joule would take us much deeper into the topic of energy than we need to go at this stage. However, it is useful for you to get a 'feel' for the size of a joule, which the domestic electric kettle can provide. A kettle can hold about two litres of water. If the kettle is well insulated to avoid heat loss, and the water is heated from 20 °C to 100 °C, then about 6.7×10^5 J – approaching one million joules – of energy are transferred from the heating element to the water. The joule is therefore a rather small unit by everyday standards.

● Describe the variation in temperature in London, shown by the dashed line in Figure 2.1.

◍ The temperature decreases very slightly for the first 8 hours; it then rises to a peak over a period of about 6 hours; after which it decreases again, steeply at first and then more gently.

● What approximate time of day in London do you think is represented by 0 hours on Figure 2.1?

◍ As the 24-hour period progresses, London will experience night for part of the time and daylight for the rest. We would expect daytime temperatures to be higher than those at night because in London in November the incoming sunlight (or more accurately the incoming solar radiation, which is considered in Section 3.2) warms up the land surface, while at night this warmth is re-radiated back into space and the land cools down. As 0 hours was during the cooler part of the period, we can infer that this represented night-time. However, note that the surface temperature stayed fairly constant during the night but was coolest at the end. This suggests that this particular night was cloudy and the clouds trapped the heat being given out by the land surface as it cooled. (We shall explore this phenomenon in more detail in Chapter 4.)

Box 2.2   Measuring temperature

Air temperature is traditionally measured using a thermometer. Typically this consists of a glass bulb filled with a liquid that expands as it gets warmer. The bulb is attached to a thin glass tube along which the expanding liquid passes. The tube has graduation marks along it so that the amount of movement of the liquid can be recorded. The marks are calibrated by placing the thermometer in situations where the temperature is known, such as the freezing point of pure water and the boiling point of pure water at a standard atmospheric pressure. On the Celsius, or centigrade, scale the freezing point of water is given the value 0 °C and the boiling point 100 °C, and the thermometer scale is divided into 100 one-degree marks. Several liquids can be used in a thermometer and the metal mercury, which is a liquid above –38.9 °C, is often used. In some parts of the world, such as Siberia, where temperatures often fall below the freezing point of mercury, other liquids such as pure alcohol (freezing point –114.4 °C) are used instead.

Maximum and minimum thermometers are designed to record the highest and lowest temperatures reached in a given period (usually 24 hours measured from 09.00 hours). In a maximum–minimum thermometer small metal markers are pushed along the graduated expansion tube by the liquid and they remain at the point where the temperature was at either the lowest or the highest. They are reset either with a magnet or by shaking the thermometer.

In many modern weather-recording stations the temperature is measured with temperature-sensitive electrical circuits, and is recorded continuously or is reported automatically by a radio signal to a data-logger.

To measure air temperature in a consistent and reliable way the thermometer should not be placed in direct sunlight and it should be in a well ventilated area. To ensure uniform conditions for taking the measurements, a standard enclosure for the thermometers is used called a Stevenson screen (Figure 2.2). This is basically a white painted box, mounted between one and two metres above the ground, with louvered sides to allow the free movement of air.

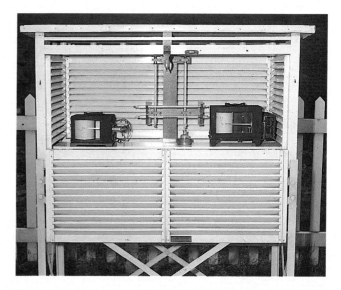

Figure 2.2   An open Stevenson screen showing thermometers (mounted centrally) and other meteorological instruments.

In addition, temperatures should not be measured too close to a building, where heat lost from the building might affect the reading. In a large town or city, the heat generated by heating and air conditioning, vehicles and electric appliances can lead to an 'urban heat island' with temperatures several degrees higher than the surrounding countryside. This effect needs to be taken into account for temperature records made in towns and cities, especially where records have been kept over a long period of time during which the 'heat island' effect has probably changed.

So, the temperature of a substance is a measure of its energy content. If you are not familiar with how temperature measurements are made and why they can be compared no matter where or when they are made, you should now read Box 2.2. After that, we shall look at global temperature measurements.

2.2   Mean surface temperature

It is obvious from Figure 2.1 that there is little daily variation in the global mean (average) surface temperature compared with the variation in London. We shall now look at averages more closely because the concept of 'average temperature' is at the heart of the issue of global warming.

- Why is there little variation in the global average surface temperature?

- When we look at temperatures around the whole globe at any instant, half of the globe is receiving sunlight and half is in darkness. As the 24-hour period progresses, the Earth's rotation means that different parts of the globe are in daylight or darkness. However, as one part heats up, another part cools down, so the average temperature of the whole Earth's surface should barely change. The small fluctuation shown in Figure 2.1 occurs because land and sea are not uniformly distributed around the globe, and land heats up and cools down more rapidly than water. These different rates cause the average surface temperature to be slightly lower when the sunlight falls mainly on sea and slightly higher when it falls mainly on land. (We shall return to this phenomenon in Chapter 3.)

The idea of 'averaging' is to give a single value that best represents a fluctuating quantity, such as temperature. In everyday speech the word 'average' can be used to describe any typical attribute of something. However, this is a rather loose definition and can sometimes lead to confusion. To overcome this problem, scientists define the term 'mean' as the sum of a series of measurements divided by the number of those measurements.

To take an actual example, Table 2.1 shows the 24 hourly surface temperature readings from 00.00 (midnight) to 23.00 (11 pm) taken on a summer's day in Milton Keynes. Rather than poring over the numbers in the table, the easiest way to get a picture of how the temperature varied throughout the day is to plot, on a graph, each temperature reading against the time it was taken, as in Figure 2.3. Before looking at the information on this graph, note how the axes are labelled. The horizontal axis is the time during the day in hours, starting at zero hours (midnight) and using the 24-hour clock.

Table 2.1   The temperature in Milton Keynes every hour from 00.00 (midnight) to 23.00 (11 pm) on a day in summertime. These data are plotted in Figure 2.3.

Time/hour	Temperature/°C	Time/hour	Temperature/°C
00.00	16.4	12.00	19.2
01.00	15.9	13.00	20.1
02.00	15.3	14.00	20.3
03.00	15.0	15.00	21.6
04.00	16.0	16.00	23.1
05.00	15.7	17.00	24.5
06.00	15.8	18.00	25.2
07.00	16.0	19.00	24.8
08.00	17.0	20.00	23.7
09.00	17.4	21.00	21.9
10.00	17.4	22.00	18.9
11.00	18.1	23.00	16.5

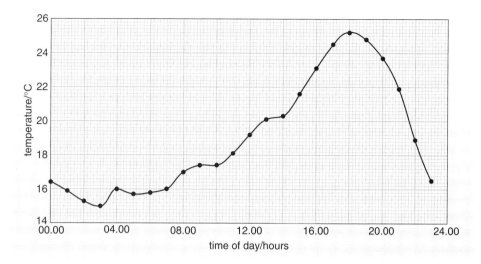

Figure 2.3 Graph showing how the surface temperature in Milton Keynes varied over a 24-hour period on a day in summertime. Each dot represents one temperature reading, at the time indicated by the horizontal axis (see Table 2.1). The curved line drawn through the points shows the overall trend more clearly and allows temperatures at times between measurements to be estimated.

● Where does the vertical (temperature) axis start, and why doesn't it start at 0 °C?

It starts at 14 °C. If it had started at 0 °C, there would have been a large empty space in the bottom half of the graph, with the plotted information occupying only the top half of the diagram. As well as being a waste of space, this would make it more difficult to read the plotted information accurately, so the scales and ranges of the axes on a graph are chosen to make the best use of the space on the page.

The graph is far more informative than the numbers in the table and immediately shows the daily cycle of warming and cooling. The peak in the graph allows us to spot quickly when the maximum temperature occurred. Likewise, the lowest temperature and its time are also easier to spot by glancing at the graph than by scanning down the columns of numbers in Table 2.1.

● What are the maximum and minimum temperatures in the 24-hour period plotted in Figure 2.3, and at what times do they occur?

The maximum temperature is 25.2 °C, which was reached at 18.00 hours or 6 pm. The minimum temperature was 15.0 °C, which was reached at 03.00 hours or 3 am.

To summarise these two extreme measurements, we can work out their mean. The definition of a mean can be expressed as an equation:

$$\text{mean} = \frac{\text{sum of the measurements}}{\text{number of measurements}} \qquad [2.1]$$

Therefore, the mean of the two extreme temperatures is:

$$\frac{(25.2\,°\text{C} + 15.0\,°\text{C})}{2} = 20.1\,°\text{C}$$

● From Table 2.1, what is the mean of all the temperature measurements in Figure 2.3?

$$\text{Mean} = \frac{\text{sum of the measurements}}{\text{number of measurements}}$$

$$= \frac{455.8\,°\text{C}}{24}$$

$$= 19.0\,°\text{C}\ \text{rounded to one decimal place.}$$

So, the mean surface temperature in Milton Keynes on this day was 19.0 °C.

The temperature measurements in Table 2.1 are all recorded to one decimal place, but what determines the number of digits recorded when we make such a measurement? Why, for example, is the first temperature recorded as 16.4 °C, rather than 16 °C or 16.42 °C? This is discussed in Box 2.3.

Box 2.3 Uncertainties

Figure 2.4 shows two thermometers which are measuring the same air temperature. Thermometer A is indicating that the temperature is between 16 °C and 17 °C, so it is 'sixteen point something' °C. The 'something' cannot be read precisely – but it is slightly less than half-way between the divisions corresponding to 16 °C and 17 °C, so we might record the temperature as 16.4 °C. We cannot be very confident about the value of this last digit; some people might record the temperature as 16.3 °C and others as 16.5 °C, rather than 16.4 °C. Even the same person reading this thermometer might at different times record the temperature as 16.4 °C or 16.5 °C or 16.3 °C. Because of the uncertainty about the digit in the first decimal place, there is clearly no point in trying to 'guess' a second decimal place here.

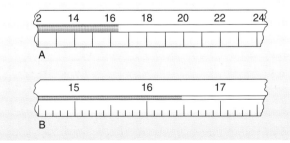

Figure 2.4 Two thermometers with different scale divisions. Both are measuring the air temperature in the same place and at the same time.

Now look at thermometer B in Figure 2.4, which has scale divisions every 0.1 °C.

● What is the temperature indicated by thermometer B?

○ The temperature is between 16.4 °C and 16.5 °C. The second decimal place is rather uncertain, but it appears to be about 7, so we could record the temperature as 16.47 °C. However, you might think the last digit should be 6 or 8, or possibly even 5 or 9.

We can indicate how well we know the value of a measured quantity by quoting explicitly the uncertainty in that value. For the temperature measured by thermometer A, we estimated that the possible range was between 16.3 °C and 16.5 °C. This means that we are fairly confident that the temperature is within 0.1 °C of 16.4 °C. The temperature could be as low as (16.4 − 0.1) °C or as high as (16.4 + 0.1) °C. This is written as 16.4 ± 0.1 °C, and we would say it is 'sixteen point four plus or minus zero point one degrees Celsius'. The temperature measured by thermometer B is written as 16.47 ± 0.02 °C, if we are confident that its reading is certainly between 16.45 and 16.49. The plus or minus quantity (± 0.1 °C in the first case and ± 0.02 °C in the second) is usually referred to as the uncertainty in the measurement. We would say that the first measurement of 16.4 °C has an uncertainty of ± 0.1 °C, and the second measurement of 16.47 °C has an uncertainty of ± 0.02 °C.

The thermometers in Figure 2.4 illustrate the uncertainties that are associated with reading a measuring instrument. However, there are other types of uncertainty in measurements that we may need to consider too. Perhaps the air temperature fluctuates on a fairly short time-scale because of variations in the wind and cloud cover, so that a series of measurements over a few minutes shows a range of values. In this case, too, we could quantify the uncertainty by stating the range of values. This type of uncertainty and the uncertainties in reading values from a scale are examples of random uncertainties, so called because the measured values are scattered fairly randomly about some mean value. We can estimate the combined effect of all the random uncertainties associated with a measurement by making the measurement several times: the spread of the results indicates the random uncertainties that are present.

There is yet another type of uncertainty in measurements that is rather more difficult to assess. We can illustrate this with the thermometer example again. The scale might be incorrectly located on the thermometer so that, for example, the temperature recorded is always 0.5 °C higher than the actual value. This causes what is known as a systematic error, or systematic uncertainty, in all of the temperatures that are recorded – they are all 0.5 °C too high. Alternatively, the Stevenson screen (Figure 2.2) may be incorrectly constructed: perhaps it is painted the wrong colour, so that it absorbs too much solar radiation, or it has too much ventilation, or it is at the wrong height from the ground. All of these factors could lead to systematic differences between the measured temperature and the temperature that would have been measured if the approved screen design had been used. These 'problems' cause systematic uncertainties in the temperatures that are recorded. In contrast to the case of random uncertainties, the presence of a systematic uncertainty is often much less obvious. In particular, making repeat measurements with the same equipment will not help because all the measurements will be affected in the same systematic way. Uncertainty will be revealed only by carefully checking the calibration of the measuring instrument against a standard that is known to be accurate. Unless this is done, a systematic uncertainty can easily remain undetected.

In the same way as we calculated a daily mean temperature, it is possible to calculate a monthly mean temperature (as in Figure 1.2a for London) or an annual mean surface temperature using measurements taken at frequent and regular intervals throughout a month or year. The procedure for calculating the annual mean surface temperature can be written as:

$$\text{annual mean surface temperature} = \frac{\text{sum of all temperature values}}{\text{number of temperature values}} \qquad [2.2]$$

● Throughout a year, the temperature at a particular location was measured at 06.00 hours and 18.00 hours every day. The sum of these temperatures is 6 647 °C. Calculate the annual mean surface temperature at this location.

◉ The number of temperature values is twice the number of days in a year, i.e. 2×365. So, using equation 2.2:

$$\text{annual mean surface temperature} = \frac{6\,647\,°C}{2 \times 365} = 9.1\,°C$$

You may have noticed that we calculated the mean surface temperature in Milton Keynes from Table 2.1, firstly, as the mean of that day's maximum and minimum temperatures and, secondly, as the mean of 24 hourly measurements, whereas in the example above we calculated a mean based on temperatures at 06.00 and 18.00 hours. If you were concerned that these means might not be equivalent, you were right! They are accurate calculations of mean temperatures, but they are means of different types of measurement: maximum and minimum in the first case, hourly measurements in the second case, and measurements at 06.00 and 18.00 in the third case. Therefore, they are subtly different. Moreover, none of these techniques indicate how long these temperatures prevailed. For instance, sunlight may have broken through the clouds only around the time that the maximum temperature was recorded, while for most of the day it was several degrees cooler. To obtain a more representative mean value, the temperature would have to be measured much more regularly than twice a day, although not necessarily as often as in Table 2.1.

Of course, no two years are identical, either because occasionally there is an unusually cold or unusually warm year or because of longer-term global warming or cooling. To avoid the vagaries of an unusual year, and to serve as a benchmark against which to judge annual mean temperatures, meteorologists have adopted a convention of calculating a 30-year mean surface temperature. As its name implies, this is arrived at in the following way.

1   The surface temperature is recorded several times a day, every day, for a period of 30 years.

2   The 30-year mean surface temperature is then calculated by adding up all the temperature values, and dividing the sum by the total number of values.

Mean monthly temperatures such as those in Figure 1.2 are also based on 30 years of readings.

By calculating a mean surface temperature, we smooth out the variability of the weather at any particular location. For example, the 30-year annual mean surface temperature in Birmingham, England, is 9.6 °C, but the highest recorded temperature there is a hot 33 °C and the lowest is a cold –12 °C. However, here our goal is to understand what determines the *mean* temperature, and not the short-term variations above and below it. Records of mean temperatures are crucial for checking climate models.

2.3 Global mean surface temperature

If we are interested in global warming, our primary concern is with the mean surface temperature averaged over the whole surface of the Earth, both land and sea – the global mean surface temperature (GMST), which you met in Chapter 1. Usually the average is over one or more years. Thus, to obtain the GMST, we need the mean surface temperature at a very large number of locations around the globe, and to work out their mean value, as follows.

$$\text{GMST} = \frac{\text{sum of all single location mean surface temperatures}}{\text{number of surface locations}} \qquad [2.3]$$

Although the GMST refers to the whole of the Earth's surface, we can show how it can be calculated from the calculation for just a portion of the Earth, e.g. the UK.

● Calculate a 30-year mean surface temperature for the UK from the data given in Figure 2.5.

◉ The sum of the mean surface temperatures is 87.3 °C and there are nine locations. Therefore, from equation 2.2:

the UK's 30-year mean surface temperature = $\frac{87.3\,°C}{9} = 9.7\,°C$

Comparing this value with the map in Figure 2.5, it looks realistic – it is higher than some of the measured temperatures and lower than others.

● What needs to be done to obtain a more representative value?

◉ A more representative value could be obtained if there were more locations, uniformly spread over the UK.

The value for the UK's 30-year mean surface temperature calculated from the data in Figure 2.5 is not as accurate as it could be. This is because the locations do not cover the country evenly: there are too many in the south and at the coast. A more representative value is 9.2 °C,

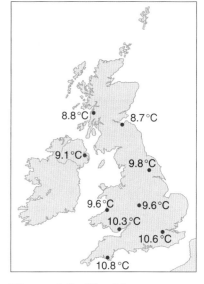

Figure 2.5 The 30-year mean surface temperature at a few locations in the UK.

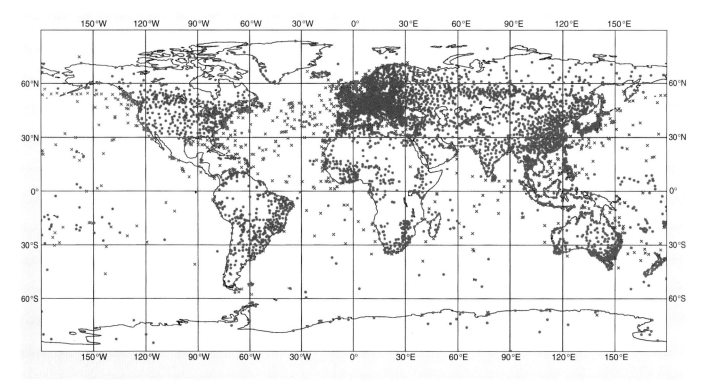

Figure 2.6 The global distribution of temperature observations on a particular day. Note the paucity of data over the oceans.

obtained from 25 weather stations distributed more evenly across the UK. For calculating the GMST, it is desirable to spread thermometers uniformly around the globe. In practice, however, the spread is not uniform, weather stations being scarce in remote cold polar regions and over the oceans. Figure 2.6 shows the actual distribution, on a particular day, of temperature readings around the globe. You can see straight away that readings over the oceans are very sparse compared with those on land and that the density of land-based readings is much higher in more populated regions. To some extent this can now be moderated by satellite data, but such data are still limited as far as 30-year means are concerned. The *apparent* distribution of readings is also affected by the map projection used (see Box 2.4). In the projection used in Figure 2.6, the polar regions look bigger than they are relative to regions closer to the Equator.

To avoid the GMST being biased towards values from densely monitored areas, a mean temperature is calculated for each region of the Earth and these mean values are combined into a single GMST. Whatever the method, finding the GMST involves a huge international effort requiring literally millions of measurements, all carefully done, documented and assessed for accuracy.

To supplement land-based temperature measurements, satellites continuously monitor global temperatures from space. This is not an easy exercise but an 18-year record (from 1981 to 1998) of global land surface temperatures shows that the Earth's snow-free land surfaces have, on average, warmed during this

Box 2.4   *Latitude, longitude and map projections*

You are probably familiar with the terms latitude and longitude, which are used for specifying locations on the Earth's surface. Figure 2.7 shows a geographical globe (a spherical map of the Earth) from two viewpoints. In Figure 2.7a, the blue lines running from left to right are lines of latitude (the Equator being one such line) and the red lines running from one pole to the other are lines of longitude. In Figure 2.7b, which is the view from above the North Pole, the circles are the lines of latitude and the lines radiating out from the pole are the lines of longitude. The unit of measurement is the degree (symbol °).

Latitude is a measure of distance north (N) or south (S) from the Equator. The Equator is 0° latitude and the North and South Poles are at +90° and −90° latitude, respectively. If you walk in a straight line north between 0° latitude and 1° N, you will cover the same distance as if you walk between 89° N and 90° N. However, if you imagine walking around the Earth along a line of latitude, you will have to walk much further to get round at the Equator than, for example, at 50°.

Longitude is a measure of how far east (E) or west (W) a location is from the Greenwich Meridian, which passes through London and defines 0° longitude. If you walk round the Equator, the distance between 80° E and 90° E is the same as between 130° E and 140° E. However, near the

poles, the lines of longitude are much closer together than at the Equator, so the distance between 80° E and 90° E is much less than it is at the Equator. Table 2.2 shows some examples of latitudes and longitudes.

Table 2.2   Examples of locations expressed as latitude and longitude. A, B and C are marked on Figure 2.7.

Tropic of Cancer	23.5° N
Tropic of Capricorn	23.5° S
Arctic Circle	66.5° N
Antarctic Circle	66.5° S
A London	51.5° N 0° W
B Cairo	30° N 30° E
C Rio de Janeiro	23° S 45° W

A map projection is an attempt to draw the surface of the three-dimensional, spherical Earth on a flat, two-dimensional piece of paper or computer screen (e.g. Figure 2.6). To do this, compromises have to be made. It is not possible to keep everything completely accurate. For example, the angle from one place to another might become distorted, or the relative size of one country with respect to another one might be wrong. In many projections, such as so-called cylindrical projections (see Figures 1.3, 1.4 and 2.6), the land is spread out sideways at the poles to fill a rectangular box neatly. This means that land masses closer to the poles (such as Greenland) appear much bigger than they really are relative to land masses nearer the Equator (such as Africa).

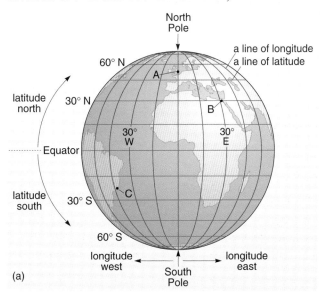

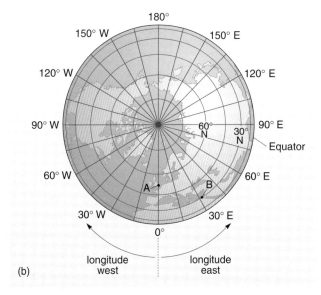

Figure 2.7   A geographical globe viewed from (a) above the Equator and (b) above the North Pole. Lines of latitude and longitude are shown at 15° intervals.

time. The satellite record is more detailed and comprehensive than previously available ground measurements because temperatures can be obtained over the whole ocean surface. However, unlike the traditional measurements that are taken in Stevenson screens at least a metre above the ground surface, satellites can measure temperatures on the ground surface itself. Thus, the two sets of measurements complement each other.

Over the 18-year period the NASA satellite data showed global average temperature increases of 0.43 °C per decade. By comparison, ground station data (air temperatures measured 2 metres above the surface) showed a rise of 0.34 °C per decade. However, not everywhere is warming uniformly. While many regions were warming, central continental regions in North America and Asia appeared to be cooling over the same period. Figure 2.8 shows the kind of data that can be collected and analysed. This image displays relative differences in temperature over Europe, comparing July 2001 with July 2003.

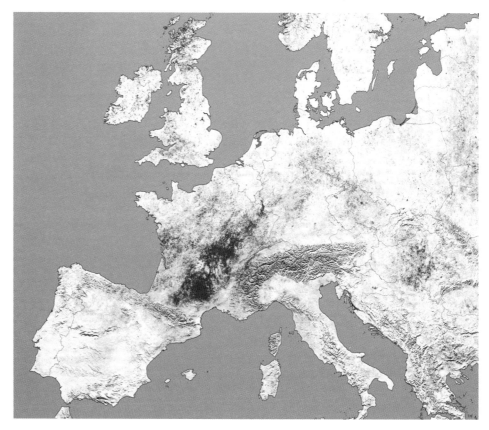

Figure 2.8 This image, based on data collected by NASA's Terra satellite, shows the differences in daytime land surface temperatures collected during the European heat wave in July 2003 compared with July 2001. The colours represent the size of the temperature differences. A blanket of deep red across southern and eastern France (left of image centre) shows where temperatures were 10 °C hotter in July 2003 than the equivalent period in 2001. White areas show where temperatures were similar, and blue shows where temperatures were cooler.

In this chapter, we have seen that temperature is a measure of the amount of kinetic energy (energy of motion) that a substance's particles have. We have seen how air temperatures can be measured, and how a worldwide set of surface temperature measurements can be combined to give the global mean surface temperature or GMST. In Chapters 3 and 4, we shall see how energy received from the Sun heats the Earth, while the radiation of energy from the Earth into space cools the Earth, and how the balance between the two changes the GMST.

2.4　Summary of Chapter 2

1　Energy is a measure of the capability of an object to make things happen. The joule is the agreed SI unit for energy.

2　The temperature of a substance indicates the energy of random motion that its constituent particles possess.

3　Daytime land surface temperatures are higher than those at night because incoming solar radiation warms up the land surface, while at night this warmth is re-radiated back into space and the land cools down. Clouds can trap the heat being given out by the land surface as it cools.

4　The mean of a set of quantities equals the sum of the values divided by the number of values.

5　Mean temperatures can be calculated for a given location or for several locations regionally, nationally or globally to give the global mean surface temperature or GMST. For a mean value to be representative of a region requires an even coverage of recording locations, but often measurements are clustered around concentrations of population or coastlines, with few in remote cold polar regions and over the oceans. To some extent this is now moderated by satellite data.

6　There are random uncertainties associated with reading a measuring instrument and measuring a quantity that fluctuates. We can estimate the combined effect of random uncertainties by making the measurement several times. There are also systematic uncertainties, which affect all of a set of measurements and cannot be estimated through making repeat measurements in the same way.

'Everybody talks about the
weather, but nobody does
anything about it.'
Mark Twain

3 Heating of the Earth by the Sun

In Chapter 2 we talked a lot about temperature. After all, temperature is one climate variable we can relate to easily, particularly because it determines how comfortable we feel. Temperature is also fundamental to the entire weather and climate system because it is a measure of the energy that powers the weather systems. Furthermore, understanding past variations in the temperature should help us to predict future ones. Our starting point is to consider the factors that determine the global mean surface temperature (GMST). The GMST depends on the various ways in which the Earth's surface both gains energy and loses energy. In this chapter we shall explore the transfer of energy between the Sun and the Earth's surface and atmosphere. You will learn what solar radiation is and what happens to the energy it carries when it reaches the Earth. We will look mostly at energy gain, while in Chapter 4 we shall examine how energy is redistributed and consider in more detail how it is lost. We start by looking broadly at these gains and losses and how they determine the GMST, but first we must discuss energy transfer: Box 3.1 introduces this concept.

Box 3.1 Power

● How was 'energy' defined in Chapter 2?

◉ It is a physical property of an object that can be transferred to another object to make things happen, e.g. cause its temperature to rise.

Like energy, 'power' is another everyday word that also has a precise scientific meaning, which is derived from the scientific concept of energy. Power is the rate at which energy transfer takes place, i.e. it is the amount of energy transferred in one unit of time. This can be expressed in words as:

power = energy transferred per unit of time

or

$$\text{power} = \frac{\text{energy transferred}}{\text{time taken}} \qquad [3.1]$$

● What unit is energy measured in?

◉ The joule (symbol J) is the SI unit of energy.

The SI unit of time is the second (symbol s), so power is the number of joules transferred per second. For example, suppose that 500 joules of energy are transferred from one object to another in 20 seconds.

Then the energy transferred per second $= \dfrac{500\,\text{J}}{20\,\text{s}} = 25$ joules per second or $25\,\text{J}\,\text{s}^{-1}$. So, in this case, the rate of energy transfer, or power, is $25\,\text{J}\,\text{s}^{-1}$.

In many circumstances it is the rate of energy transfer that matters and not the total amount transferred. For example, if we want to know how rapidly the temperature of a litre of water will rise by 1 °C, it is not enough to know that 4200 J will raise it from 20 °C to 21 °C. We need to know how rapidly the energy will be transferred, or supplied, to the water.

● If 4200 J are supplied to the water in two seconds, how long will it take for the water temperature to rise by 1 °C?

◉ As 4200 J is the amount of energy needed to raise the temperature by 1 °C and it is supplied in two seconds then the temperature rise also takes two seconds.

● What is the rate of energy supply (the power) in this case?

◉ If 4200 joules are supplied in 2 s, from equation 3.1:

$$\text{power} = \frac{4\,200\ \text{J}}{2\ \text{s}} = 2100\ \text{J s}^{-1}$$

It is rather cumbersome referring to the rate of energy transfer or power in joules per second; the watt (symbol W) is the SI unit that equals one joule per second. This is exactly the same watt that is used to specify the power requirements of electrical appliances. However, the watt is a general unit for the rate of all forms of energy transfer, not just those involving electricity.

● Express 2100 J s⁻¹ in watts.

◉ This is 2100 watts or 2100 W.

Typical domestic electric kettles have power ratings of between 1000 W and 3000 W, i.e. the electric element in a kettle will transfer energy to the water in it at a rate somewhere in this range. In the domestic setting, power is usually quoted in kilowatts (kW), where 1 kW = 1000 W.

On most kettles the power rating is displayed on the underside, e.g. 2.4 kW. The higher the power rating, the more energy per second is transferred to the water and the faster a given amount of water will boil.

● A well-insulated kettle containing two litres of water requires 6.7×10^5 J to raise the temperature of the water from 20 °C to 100 °C. If this takes 335 seconds, what is the power rating of this particular kettle? (Ignore heat losses from the water to the surrounding air and the energy required to heat the kettle itself.)

◉ From equation 3.1:

$$\text{power} = \frac{\text{energy transferred}}{\text{time taken}}$$

$$= \frac{6.7 \times 10^5\ \text{J}}{335\ \text{s}} = \frac{670\,000\ \text{J}}{335\ \text{s}} = 2000\ \text{J s}^{-1} = 2000\ \text{W} = 2\ \text{kW}$$

You are now ready to consider the various rates of energy transfer – the rates of energy gain and loss – that determine the GMST. Although 'power' is an equivalent term to 'rate of energy transfer' and is shorter, we shall normally use the longer expression because it is more descriptive.

3.1 The balance of energy gains and losses

The GMST depends on the rate at which the Earth's surface gains energy, and the rate at which it loses energy. Note that, strictly speaking, 'surface' means the actual ground (or ocean) surface but we can extend this to include the air just above it.

> The Sun is the ultimate source of almost all the energy gained by the Earth's surface.

All other sources of energy are negligible. The largest of these other sources is the heat that flows out from the interior of the Earth, but this rate of flow is 2000 times less than the rate at which the surface gains solar energy. The Earth's surface loses energy by various means, which for now can be lumped together to give one overall rate of energy loss. We thus arrive at the highly simplified picture in Figure 3.1.

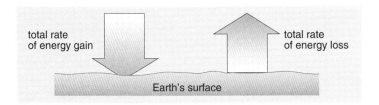

Figure 3.1 A depiction of the rates of energy gain and loss by the whole of the Earth's surface.

The downward-pointing arrow represents the rate at which the whole of the Earth's surface gains energy, and the upward-pointing arrow that originates at the Earth's surface represents the rate at which the whole of the Earth's surface loses energy. Note that in this figure the width of the downward-pointing arrow is equal to that of the upward-pointing arrow. This is a pictorial way of showing that the rates of energy gain and loss in Figure 3.1 are equal. A direct and important consequence of this equality is that the GMST in this example must be constant. If the rates were not equal then the GMST would change. Thus, if the rate of energy gain exceeded the rate of loss then the excess energy input would cause a rise in GMST to a new higher value.

- If the rate of energy loss were to exceed the rate of energy gain, what would happen to the GMST?

- The surface would cool to a lower GMST.

In reality, the rates are not exactly equal every second, and through the day and the year there are moments when the gain slightly exceeds the loss, and other moments when the loss slightly exceeds the gain. However, over a period of a few years the gains and losses largely balance out: this is why, if the GMST is averaged over a few years, the average is almost the same as over the previous or following few years. Therefore, the rates of energy gain and loss can be considered near-enough equal when averaged over this short period of time. Note that these rates can't always have been exactly equal, or the GMST would never have varied in the past, yet we know that it has (see Figure 1.5).

Let's explore in a little more detail the relationship between the GMST and the rates of energy gain and loss. This brings us to the analogy of the leaky tank. The relationship between the GMST and the rates of energy gain and loss at the Earth's surface can be thought of as behaving like a leaky tank into which water is pouring (Figure 3.2a). The rate at which water is fed into the tank from the tap represents the rate of energy gain by the Earth's surface; the rate at which water leaks out of the rectangular slot in the side of the tank represents the rate of energy loss from the Earth's surface. The level of water in the tank represents the GMST: the higher the level, the higher the GMST.

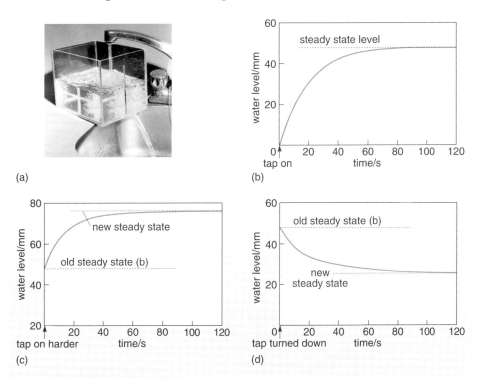

Figure 3.2 The leaky tank analogy (a); (b) to (d) graphs illustrating how the water level in the tank changes with time and for different input rates. (b) Initially the tank is empty and the water is flowing in at a certain rate. The water level rises until the leak rate increases to equal the rate of input, whereupon the level becomes steady. (c) The input rate is increased and the water rises to a new steady level that is higher. (d) The input rate is decreased and the water falls to a new steady level that is lower.

Imagine what happens if the tank is empty and the tap is turned on so the water flows in at a steady rate. We can show how the water level in the tank changes with time on the graph in Figure 3.2b. Initially, the rate of input is greater than the leak rate, so the water level rises. As the water level rises there is a greater length of slot to let the water out, and so the leak rate increases, and it continues to increase until the leak rate equals the rate of water input. At this point the water level stops rising and stays at the level it has reached. The water level is now in a steady state, i.e. the level is not changing. This equality of rates can be expressed as:

input rate = output rate   [3.2]

You can see that in the first 20 seconds after the tap is turned on, the water level rises from zero to about 30 mm. In the time interval 20 to 40 seconds after the tap is turned on, it rises from about 30 to about 43 mm, i.e. a further 13 mm in the next 20 seconds.

- How many millimetres does the water level rise in the time interval 40 to 60 seconds after the tap is turned on?

- Reading from the graph in Figure 3.2b, it rises from about 43 to about 48 mm, i.e. a further 5 mm in this next 20 seconds.

Thus, as the water level rises, the rate at which the level changes slows down. In the graph this is apparent from the line curving over. You can see that, ultimately, the line flattens out and stays at the same level – the steady state level. At this constant level the leak rate equals the rate of input.

If the tap is now turned on more to increase the input rate, the water level starts to rise again. The leak rate increases until a new steady state is reached, with a higher water level, as in Figure 3.2c. The graph shows this level to be about 76 mm. Alternatively, suppose we return to the original steady state in Figure 3.2b but reduce the flow from the tap. The leak rate is now greater than the input rate, so the water level falls. This reduces the leak rate until another steady state is reached, this time at a lower water level, as in Figure 3.2d. The graph shows this level to be 25 mm.

The leaky tank provides a simple analogy of the energy gains and losses by the Earth's surface and hence of the behaviour of the GMST. In the broadest terms, an analogy is a different type of physical system with properties that, in an important way, are similar to some of those of the actual system of interest. Analogies are often used as an aid to understanding; let's see how the analogy of the leaky tank provides insight into the behaviour of the real Earth.

In Figure 3.2b the surface of the Earth (the tank) gains solar energy (the water) and so the GMST (the water level) rises. As it does so – and this is a crucial point – the rate of energy loss from the Earth's surface increases, i.e. the higher the GMST, the greater the rate of energy loss from the Earth's surface. The reasons for this relationship between GMST and energy loss rate are explored in Chapter 4. For now, the important point is that the GMST rises until the rate of energy loss by the surface equals the rate of energy gain, whereupon, as at the right of Figure 3.2b, a steady state is reached, with the GMST no longer changing. This corresponds to the real situation in Figure 3.1.

Figure 3.2c is analogous to an increase in the rate of energy gain by the Earth's surface, such as would follow an increase in the rate at which energy is emitted by the Sun: the GMST rises until the loss rate equals the new rate of gain. We then have another situation as in Figure 3.1, but with higher gain and loss rates.

- What is happening to the GMST in the analogy in Figure 3.2d?

- In Figure 3.2d the rate of energy gain by the Earth's surface is decreased, so the GMST falls until the loss rate equals the new lower rate of gain.

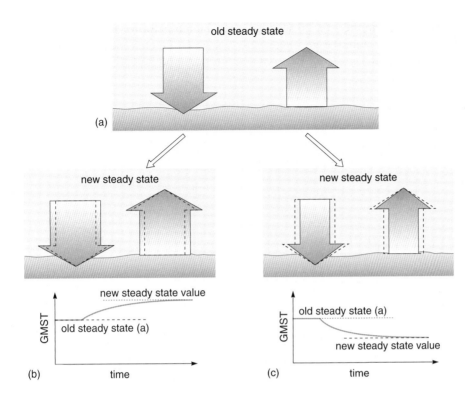

Figure 3.3 Rates of energy gain and loss, where the width of each arrow is proportional to the rate of energy transfer. (a) The old steady state. (b) When the rate of energy gain by the Earth's surface is increased, the GMST rises. (c) When the rate of energy gain by the Earth's surface is decreased, the GMST falls. The dashes in (b) and (c) show the sizes of the arrows in (a).

Figure 3.3 adds these two new steady-state cases to that in Figure 3.1, along with the graphs showing the transition of the GMST from the original steady state in Figure 3.3a to each of the new steady states.

In the water tank analogy, another way to influence the water level is to alter the width of the slot that controls the leak rate. If the slot is narrowed then the leak rate at any water level is less than it was before. If it is widened then the leak rate at any water level is higher than it was before. Widening the slot is analogous to increasing the rate of energy loss from the surface, and narrowing the slot is analogous to decreasing the rate of loss. In each case the GMST changes until a new steady state is achieved. When the loss rate is increased, the new GMST is lower and when it is decreased, the new GMST is higher.

As you will see, the processes by which the Earth's surface gains and loses energy are very different from the processes by which the tank gains and loses water. However, the analogy should help you to understand the following points.

- The rate of energy loss from the Earth's surface increases as the GMST rises, and decreases as the GMST falls.

- A steady-state GMST requires that the rate of energy gain by the Earth's surface equals the rate of energy loss.

- If the steady state is disturbed in any way, and then there is no further disturbance, a new steady state is ultimately established, with a different GMST.

3.2 Solar radiation

The Sun is the ultimate source of almost all the energy gained by the Earth's surface. Solar energy reaches us across the huge gulf of space that separates the Earth from the Sun. We sense some of this energy with our eyes as sunlight and some of it with our skin as warmth when we are in the sunshine.

3.2.1 The nature of solar radiation

The energy that floods out from the Sun is called solar radiation. There are several different types of radiation but solar radiation is dominated by an extremely important type – electromagnetic radiation. This is introduced in Box 3.2, which you need to study to understand some key ideas later in this section.

Box 3.2 Electromagnetic radiation

As its name implies, electromagnetic radiation involves electricity and magnetism, although we cannot cover exactly how here. It is conventional to divide the full range of electromagnetic radiation into sub-ranges. For example, electromagnetic radiation to which our eyes are sensitive is called visible radiation or light. Another sub-range is the electromagnetic radiation detected by our skin when we face the Sun or a fire and feel the sensation of warmth. This is called infrared radiation. Figure 3.4 shows the various sub-ranges, including these two. The order from left to right in Figure 3.4 is in accord with a property of electromagnetic radiation called the wavelength. This increases in value

continuously from left to right, with no abrupt changes from one sub-range to the next.

For something to have a wavelength it needs to be a wave. Consider the familiar example of a wave – ripples on a pond, as shown in Figure 3.5. These ripples radiate from the centre of the pattern, which could, for example, mark the point where a stone entered the water. The ripples are shown at two instants so that you can see how they move. The area marked 'wavelength' is the distance between adjacent peaks of the wave. It is also the distance between adjacent troughs.

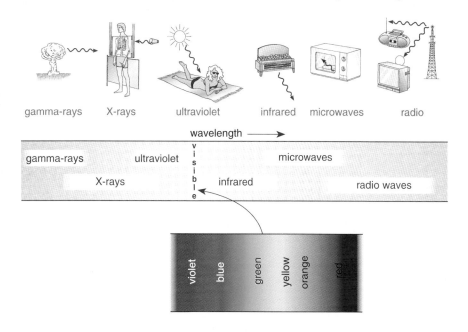

Figure 3.4
Electromagnetic radiation subdivided by wavelength. Note that the wavelength increases from left to right across the figure, so (for example) infrared has longer wavelengths than visible radiation.

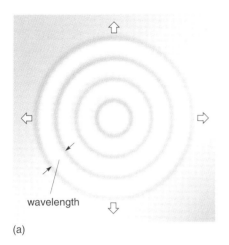

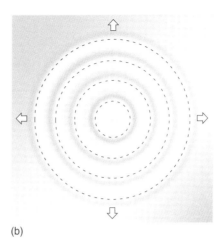

(a)

(b)

Figure 3.5 Idealised diagrams of ripples resulting from a stone being dropped into a pond at the point in the centre of the pattern: (a) shows the ripples at a particular instant; (b) shows them a short time later. The dashed circles in (b) show where the ripples were at the instant shown in (a).

In the ripples on a pond the waves are variations in the height of the surface of the water. As their name suggests, electromagnetic waves are variations in electric and magnetic effects. Although electro-magnetic radiation is a very different sort of wave from ripples on a pond, the notions of waves spreading out from a source and wavelength being a characteristic length over which the wave repeats itself still apply.

However, there is an important difference. Whereas the ripples in Figure 3.5 are waves on a surface, electromagnetic waves can spread through a volume, rather like sound waves spreading out from a loudspeaker into the surrounding air. In the case of electromagnetic waves, the volume around the source can be solid, liquid or gas, but it can also be empty space, i.e. a vacuum.

The wavelength of the ripples on a pond is usually a few centimetres. Electromagnetic waves with wavelengths of a few centimetres are known as microwaves (Figure 3.4). Radio waves are the adjacent sub-range, having longer wavelengths than microwaves. The wavelengths of visible radiation (light) are very short, around 5×10^{-7} m. A useful unit for measuring such distances is the micrometre (symbol μm), sometimes called a micron, which is 1×10^{-6} m, i.e. one-millionth of a metre.

● What is 5×10^{-7} m in micrometres?

◍ A micrometre is 1×10^{-6} m (one-millionth of a metre), so 5×10^{-7} m is 0.5×10^{-6} m, which is 0.5 μm.

Light has a range of colours which span the colours of the rainbow. These colours correspond to different wavelengths, ranging from violet light with a wavelength of about 0.4 μm to red light with a wavelength of about 0.7 μm.

● What kind of electromagnetic radiation has wavelengths between those of light and microwaves?

◍ The answer is infrared radiation (Figure 3.4).

Ultraviolet (UV) radiation has shorter wavelengths than violet visible light. Figure 3.4 also shows X-rays and gamma-rays: electromagnetic radiation with extremely short wavelengths. They will not concern us further in this book.

We need to consider the overall rate at which solar radiation reaches the Earth, so that we can explore further this dominant source of energy.

● What unit is the rate of energy transfer expressed in?

◍ The amount of energy received per unit of time, such as when the Sun is shining on a surface, is expressed as the watt, which is one joule per second or 1 J s^{-1}.

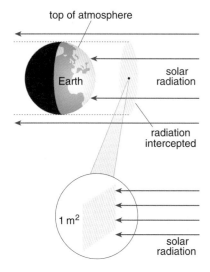

Figure 3.6 The Earth intercepts the amount of solar radiation that falls on the grey disc-shaped area facing the Sun. An area of 1 m² within this disc, shown greatly magnified at the bottom of the diagram, receives (on average) 1370 W of solar electromagnetic radiation. The Earth is much smaller than the distance to the Sun, and so the rays from the Sun are almost parallel.

A large power station generates about 10^9 W of electrical power, and all the power stations in the world generate rather less than 10^{13} W. The Sun is far more powerful: it emits electromagnetic radiation at the prodigious rate of 3.85×10^{26} W. This power is called the solar luminosity.

The radiation from the Sun spreads out in all directions. Some of it reaches the top of the Earth's atmosphere at all places on the Sun-facing side of the Earth, as in Figure 3.6. This side can be represented as a disc-shaped area facing the Sun (shown pale grey in Figure 3.6) – just as we see the full Moon as a disc in the night sky. The rate at which this area intercepts solar radiation is obtained from measurements made by radiation sensors on satellites in orbit around the Earth. (It is necessary to go into space because the Earth's atmosphere absorbs some solar radiation.) An area of one square metre facing the Sun (as in Figure 3.6) intercepts 1370 W of solar electromagnetic radiation. In other words, 1370 W per square metre, or 1370 W m^{-2}, are intercepted. This value is called the solar constant, although in reality it varies over both short time-scales (month to month, as we shall see later in this chapter) and long time-scales (e.g. geological time); 1370 W m^{-2} is a representative value.

The disc-shaped area in Figure 3.6 that the Earth presents to the Sun is 1.27×10^{14} m². The total solar radiation intercepted by the Earth can then be calculated as:

$$\text{total solar radiation intercepted} = \text{solar constant} \times \text{area of disc} \qquad \textbf{[3.3]}$$

This comes out as 1.74×10^{17} W. The total amount of solar radiation intercepted is also an average, for the same reasons that the solar constant is an average value. Not all of this intercepted radiation reaches the Earth's surface. To see why, we must examine the fate of solar radiation in its passage through the Earth's atmosphere to the surface.

3.2.2 The interaction of solar radiation with the Earth

Although the Earth's atmosphere is only a thin veneer, a few tens of kilometres thick (its vertical extent is discussed further in Chapter 5), it has significant effects on the incoming solar radiation. These effects are caused partly by the gases that constitute the atmosphere and partly by atmospheric aerosols. An aerosol is a collection of tiny liquid or solid particles dispersed in a gas, such as water droplets in the atmosphere (inside or outside clouds). Atmospheric dust is another example of an aerosol, in this case consisting of solid particles. An aerosol spray from a can consists of tiny liquid droplets. Dust and aerosols are easily seen from space (Figure 3.7) and can have a significant effect on solar radiation as it passes through the atmosphere.

Figure 3.7 This true-colour image of the North Atlantic region, taken on 4 May 2001, shows a large, thick plume of aerosols blowing eastward from North America towards Europe. The aerosol plume is the regional haze produced by the power plants and cars of the industrial northeastern USA and is typically seen during the summer months.

In its passage through the Earth's atmospheric gases and aerosols, solar radiation is subject to two different processes that each reduce the amount reaching the Earth's surface. These are contrasted in Figure 3.8a and b. The absorption of solar radiation by atmospheric gases and aerosols is shown in Figure 3.8a. The essential feature of absorption is that solar radiation is ultimately converted into heat, which causes a rise in the temperature of the atmospheric gases and aerosols.

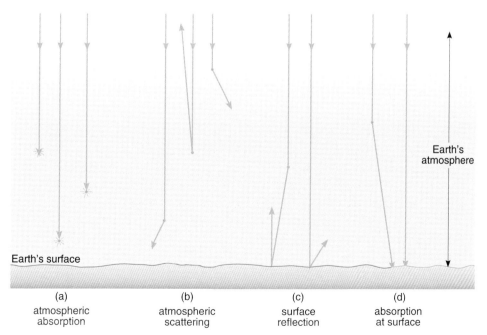

Earth's atmosphere

Earth's surface

(a)	(b)	(c)	(d)
atmospheric absorption	atmospheric scattering	surface reflection	absorption at surface

Figure 3.8 (a) The absorption of solar radiation by the Earth's atmosphere. (b) The scattering of solar radiation by the Earth's atmosphere (which causes blue skies). (c) The reflection of solar radiation by the Earth's surface. (d) The absorption of solar radiation by the Earth's surface.

Figure 3.8b illustrates another atmospheric process – scattering – in which atmospheric gases and aerosols do not absorb solar radiation but redirect it. Scattered radiation travels in all directions. Some escapes back to space and the rest reaches the Earth's surface, having taken an indirect route to get there. Clouds are particularly good scatterers but so too are some other aerosols. It is because of scattering that the sky appears bright in daytime. Since scattering redirects sunlight in all directions, a person looking at the cloudless sky in a direction away from the Sun will nevertheless see a lot of light, predominantly blue light in fact. If the atmosphere did not scatter light, the daytime sky would be as dark as it is during the night-time, as indeed it is on the Moon.

Scattering and absorption occur throughout the atmosphere, although particularly in the lower levels where most of the mass of the atmosphere is concentrated, as you will see in Chapter 5.

The solar radiation that avoids absorption or scattering back to space reaches the Earth's surface. Some of this radiation is scattered from the surface (see Figure 3.8c). In this case, because the Earth is so dense, the radiation is not scattered in all directions but only back into the atmosphere. This process is usually called reflection, although basically it is the same as scattering. Different types of surface reflect different proportions of radiation. The amount returned to space by the combined effects of scattering and reflection as a proportion of the amount arriving at that surface is called the reflectivity of the surface, also known as the albedo. Because albedo is the energy reflected as a proportion of that received, it varies between zero (in other words, all the energy is absorbed) and 1 (where all the energy is reflected and none is absorbed). Surfaces with a high reflectivity, such as snow and ice, reflect most of the solar radiation that falls on them and so have a high albedo, while oceans and surfaces covered in vegetation have a low reflectivity and hence a low albedo. All clouds are highly reflective, appearing white when illuminated (they only look grey when their undersides are in shadow). The veil-like structure of cirrus clouds means that they have a fairly low albedo of less than 0.2, while stratocumulus and cumulonimbus, which are thicker and consist of more densely packed droplets and/or ice crystals, have fairly high albedos of about 0.5 and 0.7, respectively. (Cloud types are discussed in Chapter 5.) Some typical albedo values of different surfaces are given in Table 3.1. Note that, in practice, precise values cannot be given because a surface's reflectivity depends not only on what it is made of, its colour and its roughness, but also on the angle of the incoming radiation and the wavelength of the radiation in question.

The radiation reaching the Earth's surface that is not reflected or scattered is absorbed (Figure 3.8d). In the oceans this absorption occurs throughout the top few tens of metres of water, whereas on land it is confined to a much thinner surface layer. Just as in the atmosphere, the absorbed solar radiation increases the temperature of the surface. In other words, the Earth's surface is radiantly heated by the Sun.

Table 3.1 Some typical albedo values. (The albedo can also be expressed as a percentage, i.e. by multiplying these values by 100.)

Type of surface	Albedo*
cloud	average 0.55 (0.15–0.8, depending on type and thickness)
fresh snow and sea-ice	0.8–0.9 (depending on purity, compaction and depth)
thawing snow	0.45
desert	0.35
grassland	0.25–0.33
forest, bare soil, cities	0.10–0.20

water:
    Sun high in the sky
    (elevation >40°)
	<0.05

Sun low in the sky (elevation c. 10°)	>0.5

* < means 'less than'; > means 'greater than'.

- How would you expect the visual brightness of a region in Figure 3.9 to depend on the proportion of visible solar radiation reflected or scattered by the materials in that region?

- The greater the proportion of visible solar radiation that a region reflects or scatters, the brighter the visual appearance of that region.

- From your general knowledge of the Earth, what are the brightly reflecting (high albedo) materials at locations A and B, and what is the dark (low albedo) material at location C in Figure 3.9?

- The bright material at A is cloud over the equatorial region, whereas at B it is snow, ice and cloud over Antarctica. The dark material at C is water (the Atlantic Ocean), seen through a break in the clouds.

- The large land mass in the upper-left quarter of Figure 3.9 is the continent of Africa. The northernmost and southernmost regions are light brown, while the central regions appear dark (where they are not covered in cloud). Are the albedo values in Table 3.1 consistent with what you know about African geography?

- The northernmost part of Africa is dominated by the Sahara Desert which, according to Table 3.1, should have an albedo around 0.35. Southern Africa also has desert regions. Central Africa, on the other hand, lies in the equatorial zone where there are no deserts, but instead there is much more

Figure 3.9 The Earth from space. This image was formed from solar radiation at visible wavelengths that has been scattered by clouds and reflected by the surface.

vegetation (see Figure 1.4). According to Table 3.1, the albedo of this region should be lower, in the range of 0.10 to 0.33. This is consistent with what we can see in the satellite image, where Central Africa appears much darker than the desert regions.

Figure 3.10 shows estimates of the average rates of energy transfer that involve solar radiation in the Earth's atmosphere and at the surface. In all cases average global totals are shown, i.e. the global totals averaged over several years. We could have given the values in watts, but the numbers are more manageable in Figure 3.10 if we use an arbitrary unit of power, with 100 units representing the total power in the solar radiation intercepted by the Earth.

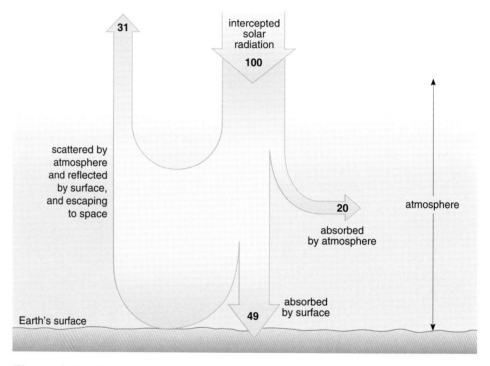

Figure 3.10 Rates of energy transfer involving solar radiation in the Earth's atmosphere, and at the Earth's surface. The width of each arrow is proportional to the rate of energy transfer. The numbers give the proportion of the incoming solar energy that is transferred by each of the four pathways.

● How many watts do 100 units correspond to in Figure 3.10?

◉ 100 units is the total incoming solar radiation which corresponds to 1.74×10^{17} watts (see Section 3.2.1).

In Figure 3.10, the arrow that sweeps through the atmosphere down to the Earth's surface and returns to space represents the rate at which solar radiation is returned to space through the combined effects of scattering by the whole depth of the atmosphere and reflection by the whole surface (31 units). The arrow that ends in the atmosphere represents the rate at which solar radiation is absorbed by the atmosphere (20 units). (This includes any scattered and reflected radiation that is subsequently absorbed by the atmosphere.) The remaining arrow represents the rate at which solar radiation is absorbed by the Earth's surface (49 units).

- What is the average albedo of the Earth based on Figure 3.10? Express your answer both as a percentage and as a decimal.

◉ The proportion of incoming radiation returned to space is 31 units and the amount received is 100 units, so the average planetary albedo is $\frac{31}{100}$ or 31% or 0.31.

In Section 3.2.1 you saw that the average amount of solar radiation intersected by a disc facing the Sun above the Earth's atmosphere, i.e. the solar constant, is 1370 W m^{-2}. However, the Earth is not a flat disc but a sphere, so the surface area receiving solar radiation is four times as great (Figure 3.11a shows why). Therefore, the average effective amount of solar radiation received per square metre of the Earth (known as the average solar flux) is only one-quarter of the solar constant, i.e. about 343 W m^{-2}. Given that the Earth's average albedo is about 0.31 or 31% (see Figure 3.10), the energy that the Earth–atmosphere system receives, and which therefore powers the Earth's weather system and all life processes, is 69% of 343, i.e. 237 W m^{-2}. Note, though, that this radiation is not uniformly distributed. Figure 3.11b shows that any cylindrical beam of solar radiation covers more of the Earth's surface at higher latitudes than it does at the Equator, so its energy is spread out over a larger area. This means that the intensity of solar radiation at the Earth's surface (the number of rays per unit area on Figure 3.11b) is less at high latitudes (polar regions) than at low latitudes (equatorial regions). Consequently, the equatorial regions are warmer than the polar regions.

The uneven heating of the Earth's surface drives the weather and the climate system.

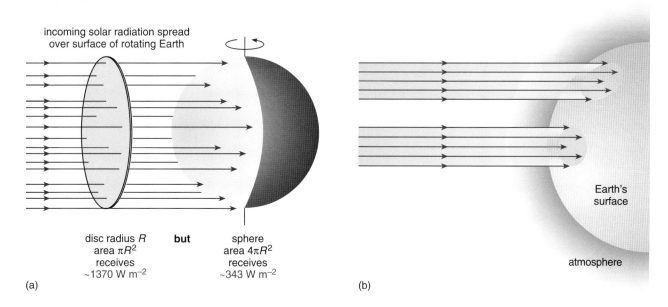

(a)
incoming solar radiation spread over surface of rotating Earth

disc radius R area πR^2 receives ~1370 W m^{-2} **but** sphere area $4\pi R^2$ receives ~343 W m^{-2}

(b)
Earth's surface

atmosphere

Figure 3.11 (a) Diagram showing the calculation of the average effective amount of solar radiation reaching the Earth – the average solar flux (~ means approximately). (b) Schematic diagram showing why there is a difference in the intensity of solar radiation reaching the Earth at different latitudes.

Of course, although the Earth as a whole intercepts more or less the same amount of solar radiation from day to day, the amount received at any point on the Earth's surface varies dramatically because the Earth rotates on its axis once every 24 hours. From the point of view of a person standing anywhere on the Earth's surface, the Sun appears to rise, travel across the sky and set. The angle at which solar radiation hits the Earth's surface at any one point is therefore constantly changing and, consequently, so is the amount of energy arriving at that surface by direct solar radiation. Figure 3.12 shows the temperatures for part of the globe at four times during a day. You can see the effect of the apparent passage of solar radiation as the Earth rotates.

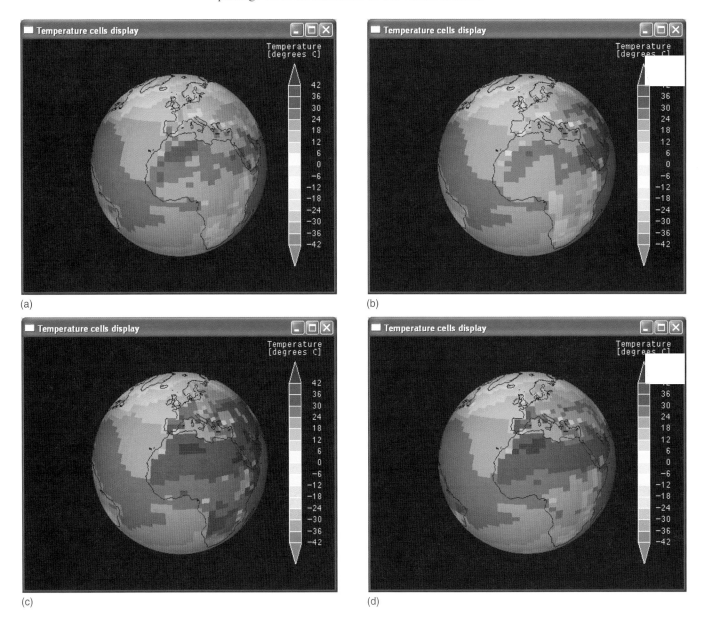

Figure 3.12 Modelled global temperatures at (a) midnight, (b) 06.00, (c) 12.00 and (d) 18.00 hours Greenwich Mean Time (GMT). The maximum temperature usually occurs in the early afternoon. On land, especially in the centre of large continents, there is a greater range of temperatures during a day than over water.

As we have seen, the amount of radiation reflected by a surface depends on the albedo of that surface and this also changes with the angle at which solar radiation strikes it. A further complication is that surfaces absorb, retain and re-radiate heat at different rates, depending on the properties of the material. Land, for example, heats up and cools down faster than water. Because water 'holds on' to the heat it absorbs, we say that it has a greater heat capacity than land. The heat capacity of a substance is the amount of heat required to change its temperature by one degree, and has units of energy per degree. The heat capacity depends on the nature of the substance as well as the amount of the substance. Therefore, a more useful measure is the specific heat capacity, which in SI units is the amount of energy in joules that is required to raise the temperature of 1 kilogram of the substance by 1 °C ($J\ kg^{-1}\ °C^{-1}$). (Strictly, the SI unit of temperature is kelvin, not Celsius, but the distinction is unimportant here.)

Just as energy is supplied to raise the temperature of 1 kilogram of a substance by 1 °C, the same amount of energy is released when 1 kilogram of that substance cools by 1 °C. Pure water has a specific heat capacity of 4184 $J\ kg^{-1}\ °C^{-1}$ whereas the rock granite (representing land) has a specific heat capacity of 790 $J\ kg^{-1}\ °C^{-1}$. This means that more energy is required to heat 1 kilogram of water by 1 °C than 1 kilogram of rock by 1 °C, so water warms up more slowly than land for a given input of energy (e.g. heat from the Sun) and also cools down more slowly.

The atmosphere also has a lower heat capacity than the oceans. In fact, the entire heat capacity of the atmosphere is equivalent to the heat capacity of just the uppermost 3 metres or so of sea water – and ocean depths extend down to several kilometres.

The oceans are a very important component of the climate system.

3.3 Annual variations in solar radiation

In Section 3.2 we said that the Earth as a whole intercepts 'more or less' the same amount of solar energy on a daily basis. The words 'more or less' were used deliberately because the amount of solar radiation reaching the Earth does in fact vary. These variations occur over a range of time-scales and we shall now look in more detail at this unevenness of heating over time. In this section we look at annual variations and in Section 3.4 we go on to consider longer-term variations.

Anyone living away from the equatorial regions of the Earth has experienced the annual cycle of the seasons. You probably know that they result from the Earth's axis of rotation being tilted relative to the plane of the Earth's orbit around the Sun. Figure 3.13 shows the hypothetical situation in which the Earth's axis of rotation is at right-angles to the plane of its orbit.

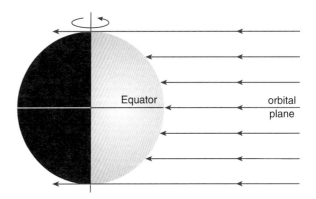

Figure 3.13 Hypothetical situation in which the Earth's axis of rotation is at right-angles to the plane of its orbit around the Sun. (Note that at the poles the Sun's rays graze the Earth's surface.)

● What are the implications of the situation in Figure 3.13 for the lengths of night and day?

◍ Night and day would always be the same length (i.e. 12 hours each) everywhere around the globe, except at the poles, which would have perpetual twilight.

In reality, the Earth's axis of rotation is tilted with respect to the plane of its orbit, currently at an angle of 23.4° (see Figure 3.14a). As a result, the noonday Sun is overhead at the Equator only twice a year – at the equinoxes, i.e. 21 March and 21 September, which is when the lengths of night and day are equal. At other times, the latitude at which the noonday Sun is overhead moves between 23.4° N (the Tropic of Cancer) and 23.4° S (the Tropic of Capricorn) and back again (Figure 3.14b). This change in the position of the noonday Sun throughout the year causes the seasons.

Figure 3.14a shows the passage of the seasons for the Northern Hemisphere. Along the Tropic of Cancer, the noonday Sun is overhead, and maximum solar radiation is received, during the summer solstice on 21 June, which is the longest day in the Northern Hemisphere. After that, the days begin to shorten. At the autumn equinox – on 21 September – day and night are of equal length. Day lengths continue to shorten until the shortest day – the winter solstice, on 21 December in the Northern Hemisphere – after which days begin to lengthen again.

The Equator receives maximum solar radiation at the March and September equinoxes, when the noonday Sun is overhead, and day and night are of equal length. Poleward of the tropics, the Sun is never overhead, although it is at its highest elevation (the angle between the Sun and the horizon) at the summer solstice (Figure 3.14c). The poles are continuously illuminated in summer, giving rise to 'the midnight Sun', whereas in winter the Sun does not appear above the horizon.

As you saw in Figure 3.11b, the angle the Sun's rays make with the Earth's surface affects the intensity of the solar radiation, which in turn affects the heating of the surface.

Figure 3.14 (a) The four seasons of the Northern Hemisphere in relation to the Earth's orbit around the Sun. The Earth's axis is tilted at approximately 23.4° to a line at right-angles to the plane of its orbit around the Sun. (b) The angle of tilt of the Earth's axis (at present 23.4°) determines the latitude of the tropics (where the Sun is overhead at one of the solstices) and of the Arctic and Antarctic Circles (66.6°, which is 90° minus 23.4°). (c) The passage of the seasons shown in terms of the position of the noonday Sun in relation to the Earth: (1) the noonday Sun overhead the Tropic of Cancer, i.e. the northern summer solstice (cf. b); (3) the noonday Sun overhead the Tropic of Capricorn, i.e. the southern summer solstice; (2) and (4) at the equinoxes, by contrast, the Sun is overhead the Equator, and the Northern and Southern Hemispheres are illuminated equally; days and nights are the same duration at all latitudes except at the poles, which are grazed by the Sun's rays for 24 hours.

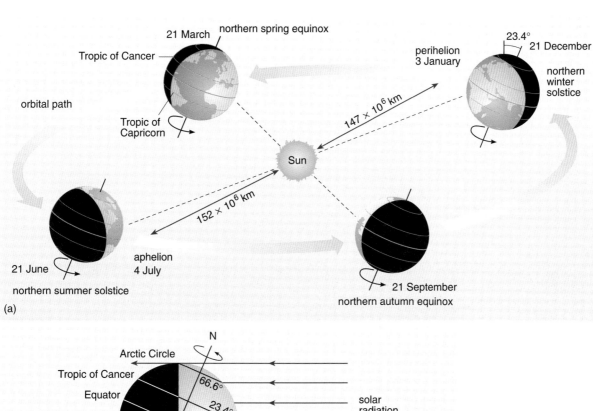

21 March

northern spring equinox

Tropic of Cancer

perihelion
3 January

23.4°   21 December

northern
winter
solstice

orbital path

147×10^6 km

Tropic of
Capricorn

Sun

152×10^6 km

21 June

aphelion
4 July

northern summer solstice

21 September

northern autumn equinox

(a)

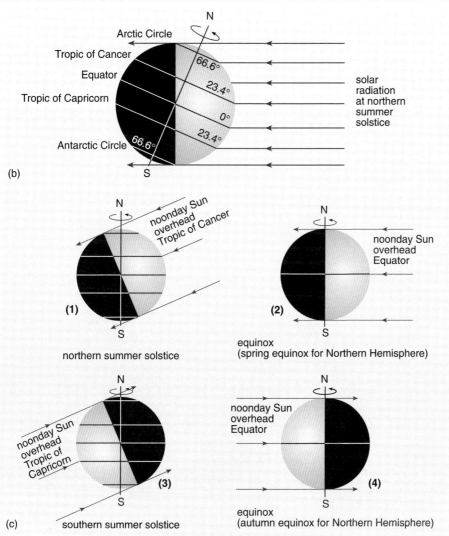

N

Arctic Circle

Tropic of Cancer

66.6°

Equator

23.4°

solar
radiation
at northern
summer
solstice

Tropic of Capricorn

0°

23.4°

Antarctic Circle   66.6°

S

(b)

N

noonday Sun
overhead
Tropic of Cancer

N

noonday Sun
overhead
Equator

(1)

(2)

S

S

northern summer solstice

equinox
(spring equinox for Northern Hemisphere)

N

N

noonday Sun
overhead
Equator

noonday Sun
overhead
Tropic of
Capricorn

(3)

(4)

S

S

(c)

southern summer solstice

equinox
(autumn equinox for Northern Hemisphere)

- How does surface temperature vary with the seasons at the tropics and at the Equator?

- At the tropics the noonday Sun is overhead at the summer solstice (Figure 3.14c), giving the highest temperatures, which then drop to a low at the winter solstice. Although the noonday Sun is exactly overhead at the Equator only at the equinoxes, it is fairly high in the sky all year round, so there is less variation in temperature than at the tropics.

Figure 3.15 shows the seasonal variations in temperature in a vertical slice through the atmosphere along a latitudinal band at 45° N (a) as a series of peaks and troughs, compared with a similar slice at the Equator (b) where there is very little seasonal variation.

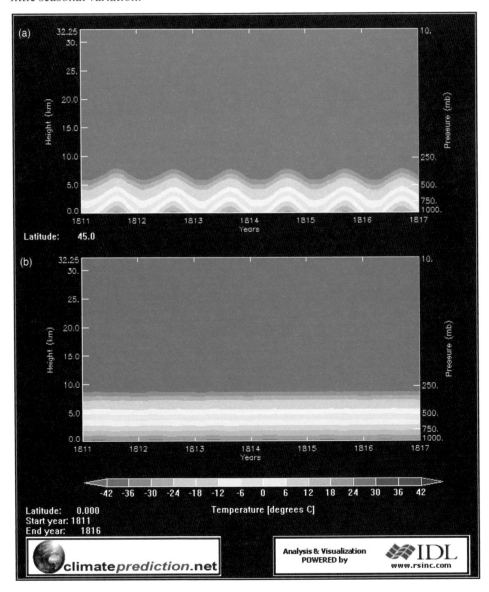

Figure 3.15 Modelled variation in temperature of the atmosphere with height (vertical axis) and time (horizontal axis) over a six-year period at (a) 45° N and (b) the Equator.

Seasonal variation in the distribution of solar radiation (both heat and light) also greatly affects the growth of vegetation, particularly at middle and high latitudes. This – along with the amount of snow, ice and cloud – in turn affects the average albedo in each hemisphere. In Figure 3.16 you can clearly see the seasonal effect on vegetation and the advance and retreat of the snow line. From December to February (the northern winter) snow covers much of northern Europe and North America. However, most of this snow disappears, at least from low-lying areas, in June to August (the northern summer). At the same time, snow accumulates in the southernmost regions of South America and the South Island of New Zealand during the southern winter.

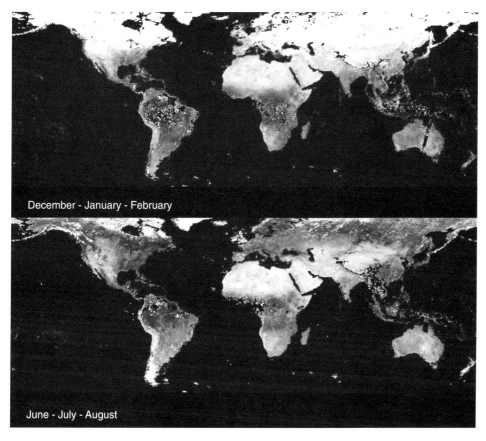

December - January - February

June - July - August

Figure 3.16 Seasonal summaries obtained by satellites of the directional hemispherical reflectance (DHR), which is the albedo in the visual parts of the electromagnetic spectrum compensated for atmospheric scattering. The images were cropped to include only the area which is illuminated in both hemispheres during winter and summer.

The seasonal variation in the amount of solar radiation received daily at the Earth's surface is shown in Figure 3.17. This is a plot in which similar values of solar radiation at different latitudes (vertical axis) and times (horizontal axis) are joined up by lines known as contours. The zero contour corresponds to 24-hour darkness. At the North Pole (90° N), it encompasses the period between 21 September and 21 March and, at the South Pole, it encompasses the period between 21 March and 21 September. In both cases, the first date is the autumn equinox and the second is the spring equinox (compare this with Figure 3.14).

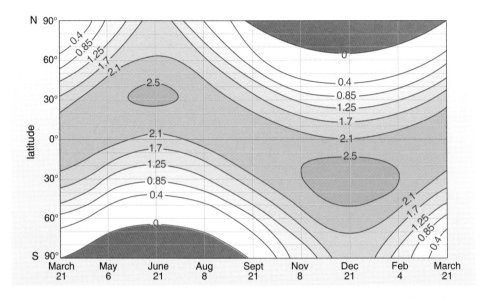

Figure 3.17 Seasonal variation of daily incoming solar radiation (in 10^7 J m^{-2} day^{-1}) at the Earth's surface, taking account of absorption by the atmosphere but ignoring the effect of topography. Note: this is not a map but a plot of contours of incoming solar radiation against latitude on the vertical axis and time of year on the horizontal axis.

● Describe briefly how the incoming solar radiation changes over the course of the year at 50° N (the latitude of southern regions of the British Isles and Canada). (To answer this, work along the line representing 50° N latitude on the vertical axis and note which contours you cross as you progress through the dates indicated on the horizontal axis.)

◐ At 50° N, the incoming solar radiation on 21 March (the spring equinox) is about 1×10^7 J m^{-2} day^{-1}; it increases up to a maximum of more than 2.1×10^7 J m^{-2} day^{-1} in late June (around the time of the summer solstice or the longest day), then declines to less than 0.4×10^7 J m^{-2} day^{-1} towards the end of December (around the time of the winter solstice or the shortest day), after which it begins to rise again.

- The units used in Figure 3.17 are J m^{-2} day^{-1} because they are values of incoming solar radiation falling on one square metre per day. How would you convert the contour values so that they gave the average incoming solar radiation in W m^{-2}?

- Watts are joules per second, therefore to convert J m^{-2} day^{-1} (incoming solar energy per square metre per day) to W m^{-2} (average power received per square metre) we must divide the contour values by the number of seconds in a day, i.e. by $24 \times 60 \times 60$ s day^{-1} = 8.64×10^4 s day^{-1}. The contour values

  would therefore range from $\dfrac{0.4 \times 10^7 \text{ J m}^{-2}\text{day}^{-1}}{8.64 \times 10^4 \text{ s day}^{-1}}$ to $\dfrac{2.5 \times 10^7 \text{ J m}^{-2} \text{ day}^{-1}}{8.64 \times 10^4 \text{ s day}^{-1}}$

  or about 46 to 289 W m^{-2}.

- Figure 3.17 shows that on average, over the year as a whole, the Equator receives the most solar radiation. Which part(s) receive the most at any one time? Can you suggest the reason for this?

- Mid-latitudes (i.e. around 30°) receive the most solar radiation at any one time: more than 2.5×10^7 J m^{-2} day^{-1} in summer; this is because of long day lengths at a time of year when the noonday Sun is high.

Note from Figure 3.17 that the maximum amount of solar energy received by southern mid-latitudes in the southern summer is greater than the maximum amount received by northern mid-latitudes in the northern summer – compare, for example, the areas enclosed by the contour for 2.5×10^7 J m^{-2} day^{-1}. Furthermore, if you study Figure 3.17 carefully you will see that in the southern summer all latitudes receive more energy than the corresponding latitudes in the other hemisphere in the northern summer. This is because the Earth's orbit around the Sun is elliptical (rather like a squashed circle). At the present time, the Earth is closest to the Sun (i.e. is at perihelion) during the southern summer (on 3 January) and is furthest from the Sun (i.e. is at aphelion) during the northern summer (on 4 July) – see Figure 3.14a.

3.4 Long-term variations in solar radiation

So far in this chapter we have discussed diurnal and annual variations in the Earth's position and orientation relative to the Sun, which lead to variations in the amount of solar radiation received by a point on the Earth's surface. These are caused by the daily rotation of the Earth (Figure 3.12), seasonal variations as a result of the Earth's axis being tilted by 23.4° relative to the orbital plane (Figures 3.14 and 3.15), and the elliptical shape of the Earth's orbit (Figures 3.14a and 3.17). There are also three much longer-term cyclical variations that affect the solar flux received at a point on the Earth's surface, which act over periods of 110 000, 40 000 and 22 000 years, and hence are significant for long-term climate change. They arise because the shape of the Earth's orbit around the Sun and its tilt relative to the orbital plane change with time. These three astronomical cycles, usually known as Milankovich–Croll cycles, are described in more detail in Box 3.3, although the precise details need not concern us here.

Box 3.3 Milankovich–Croll cycles

The varying combined gravitational attraction of the Sun and the other planets (notably Jupiter and Saturn) means the elliptical shape (known as eccentricity) of the Earth's orbit varies with time. Over a period of about 110 000 years it changes from its most elliptical (maximum eccentricity) to nearly circular and back again (Figure 3.18a). An elliptical orbit tends to exaggerate the seasons in one hemisphere and to moderate them in the other; they are more extreme for the hemisphere where winter occurs during aphelion and summer occurs during perihelion (see Figures 3.14a and 3.17). This 110 000-year cycle is the longest of the astronomical cycles that affect the amount and distribution of solar radiation reaching the Earth's surface.

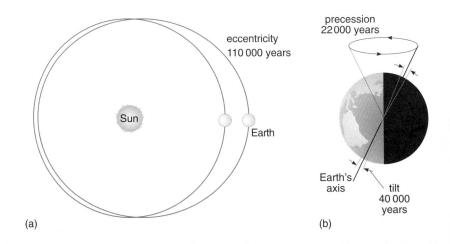

Figure 3.18 The component Milankovich–Croll cycles. The sizes of the effects are exaggerated for the sake of clarity. (a) Plan view (i.e. from the North Pole) of the Earth's orbit to show that it changes shape from its most elliptical to nearly circular and back again during the 110 000-year eccentricity cycle. (b) The Earth showing the 40 000-year tilt cycle and the 22 000-year precession cycle.

The two shorter cycles (see Figure 3.18b) involve the orientation of the Earth's axis, so they only affect the distribution of solar radiation over the Earth's surface, not the total amount received. Over a period of about 22 000 years, the direction in which the Earth's axis points traces a circle in space. This phenomenon is often referred to as the precession of the equinoxes. In addition, the angle between the axis and the direction perpendicular to the orbital plane varies between about 21.8° and 24.4°, and back again, with a periodicity of about 40 000 years. Currently the angle of tilt (often referred to as obliquity) is about 23.4° – the greater the tilt, the greater the difference between winter and summer.

The form of the three cycles over the past 800 000 years is shown in Figure 3.19.

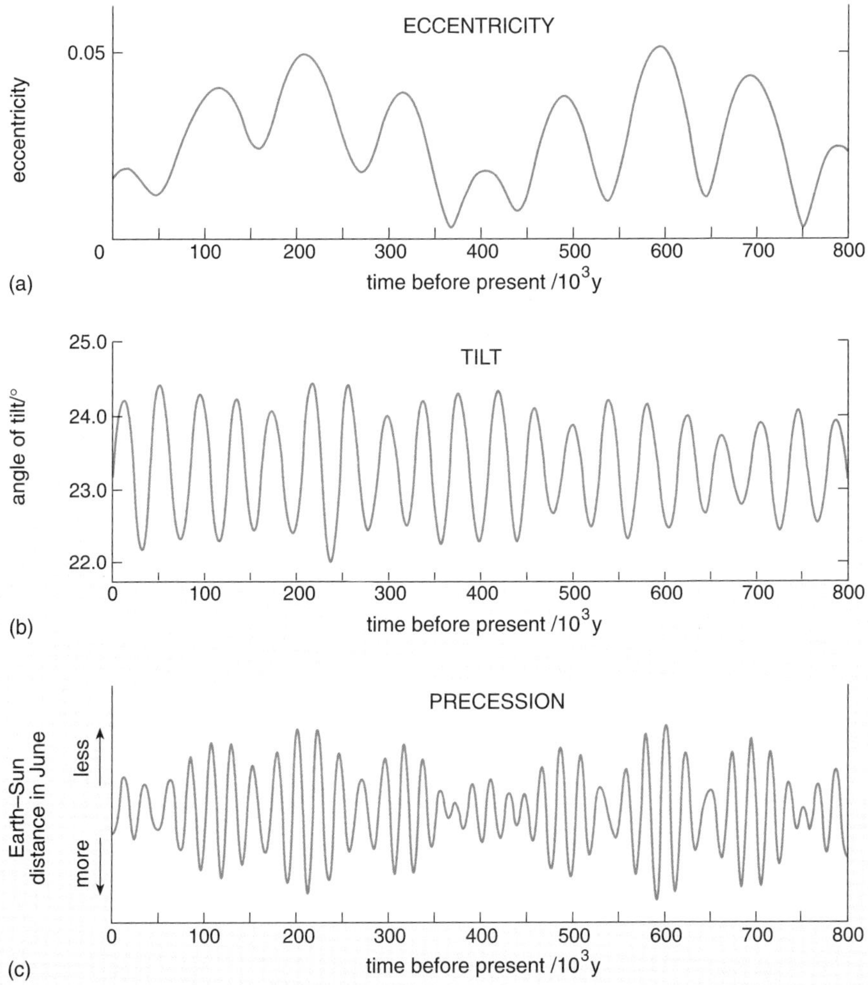

Figure 3.19 Milankovich–Croll orbital changes over the past 800 000 years, based on astronomical data. (a) Variations in eccentricity: the higher the value, the more elliptical the orbit; an eccentricity of zero corresponds to circular. (b) Variations in the angle of tilt (obliquity). (c) Precession expressed in terms of the Earth–Sun distance in June.

- What do you think the latitude of the tropics would be if the angle of tilt increased to 24.4°, rather than the present value of 23.4°? What effect would that have on a diagram such as Figure 3.17?

- If the angle of tilt increased to 24.4°, the tropics (where the Sun is directly overhead at the summer solstice) would be at 24.4° N and 24.4° S. On a diagram such as Figure 3.17 this would mean the areas of maximum incoming solar radiation corresponding to summer months would shift slightly polewards and, for the winter hemisphere, the zero contour (for example) would extend a little further towards the Equator.

Figure 3.20 is a curve computed by combining the Milankovich–Croll cycles of variations (described in Box 3.3) to show how the intensity of summer sunshine at high northern latitudes (65° N) has varied in response to orbital changes over the past 600 000 years. However, the complexity of the climate system and interactions between the different components mean that it is difficult to predict the effect of a given change in incoming solar radiation. There is good geological evidence that Milankovich–Croll cycles have been important agents of climatic variation for at least the past 2.5 million years. Furthermore, climatic changes influenced, or even triggered, by changes in incoming solar radiation associated with the Milankovich–Croll cycles could occur over a fairly short time-scale of hundreds or even tens of years. One way in which astronomical variations may affect the Earth's climate is through their influence on the growth and decay of the polar ice-caps and hence the amount of solar radiation reflected by the Earth.

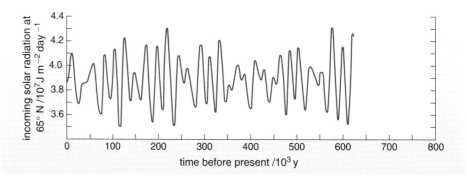

Figure 3.20 Variations in incoming solar radiation in summer at northern latitudes (65° N) over the past 600 000 years caused by Milankovich–Croll cycles.

3.5   Variation of the solar luminosity

So far we have not considered whether the intensity of radiation emitted by the Sun remains constant. Calculations of how a star ages indicate that the amount of radiation emitted by the Sun at the formation of the Solar System 4600 million years (Ma) ago was only 70 to 75% of what it is now (see Figure 3.21).

On a much shorter time-scale, there are variations in solar activity and hence luminosity on an 11-year cycle (Figure 3.22a). One manifestation of high solar activity is an increase in the number of sunspots. Sunspot cycles have been

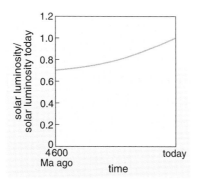

Figure 3.21 Graph showing the change in solar luminosity since the origin of the Earth 4600 Ma ago, based on the evolution of stars and expressed as a proportion of the present-day solar luminosity.

observed and recorded for hundreds of years. Although sunspots are actually darker, cooler areas of the Sun's surface (Figure 3.23a overleaf), peaks in the number of sunspots are accompanied by peaks in the numbers of 'faculae' – bright, hot areas of the Sun – whose effect outweighs that of sunspots (Figure 3.22b). Faculae become visible when the X-ray emission of the Sun is photographed (Figure 3.23b).

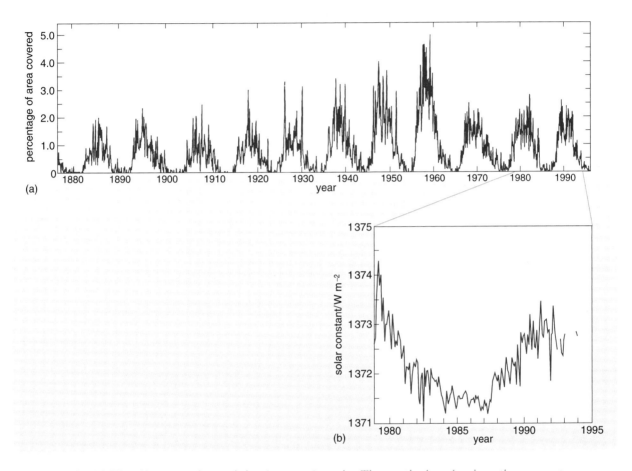

(a)

(b)

Figure 3.22 (a) The 11-year solar activity (sunspot) cycle. The vertical scale gives the percentage of the Sun's surface area covered by sunspots. (b) The variation in the solar constant (the rate at which solar radiation arrives per square metre at the top of the atmosphere), as measured by satellite-borne radiometers between 1979 and 1995. Note the rough correlation between the two traces, with minimum values around 1985–87 and maximum values about five years either side.

● According to Figure 3.22b, by approximately how much did the solar constant vary between 1979 (near the peak of a sunspot cycle) and the minimum value in mid-1982? (Express your answer as a percentage of the 1982 value.)

◎ The peak in 1979 was about 1374.3 W m^{-2} and the minimum value in 1982 was just over 1371 W m^{-2}. The difference between these two is about 3.3 W m^{-2}, which as a percentage of the 1982 value is $\frac{3.3}{1371} \times 100\%$, which is about 0.2% of the 1982 value.

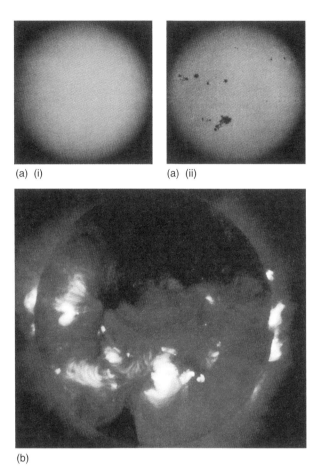

(a) (i)   (a) (ii)

(b)

Figure 3.23 (a) The Sun near a time of (i) minimum solar activity and (ii) maximum solar activity, both photographed using the visible spectrum. (b) The Sun in an active period, photographed using X-rays, which are generated by energetic activity and high temperatures in the Sun's atmosphere.

Therefore, the changes in the amount of solar radiation reaching the Earth within an 11-year cycle are relatively small. Furthermore, the fluctuations occur on such a short time-scale that the components of the climate system that respond on longer time-scales – the oceans or the polar ice-caps, for example – seem unlikely to be affected by them. However, the 11-year cycle is only part of the picture. Figure 3.22a shows clearly that the individual cycles vary slightly from one to another, having different numbers of sunspots and being of very slightly different lengths. It seems that sunspot peaks such as those in Figure 3.22a 'wax and wane' with a periodicity of 80 to 90 years; in other words, the high sunspot peaks of the middle decades of the 20th century mark the maximum of a cycle that began around 1905. Assuming that the approximate correlation between sunspot numbers and the solar constant holds good during periods of both minimum activity and maximum activity (Figure 3.22b), the solar constant must on average be greater during 'more active' cycles than during 'less active' cycles.

3.6 Summary of Chapter 3

1   The transfer of energy to an object can have a variety of effects. One of these is to cause a rise in the temperature of the object.

2   Power is the rate of energy transfer. The SI unit for energy is the joule (J) and the SI unit for power is the joule per second ($J\ s^{-1}$), which is also called the watt (W).

3   The GMST depends on the rate at which the Earth's surface gains energy and the rate at which it loses energy. If these two rates are equal then there is a steady state and the GMST will not change. If the rates are unequal then the GMST will change. The rate of loss of energy from the Earth's surface increases as the GMST rises and decreases as the GMST falls.

4   A leaky tank of water is a useful analogy for the energy gains and losses at the Earth's surface and the corresponding GMST.

5   The Sun is the ultimate source of almost all of the energy gained by the Earth's surface.

6   The amount of solar radiation that warms the surface of the Earth depends on the albedo – the proportion reflected and scattered – of the atmosphere and the Earth's surface.

7   The amount of solar radiation reaching the Earth depends on both details of the Earth's orbit (which gives us the seasons and day and night, as well as much longer time-scale changes in climate) and how solar activity changes the Sun's luminosity. The Milankovich–Croll cycles have been important agents of climatic variation for at least the past 2.5 million years.

8   More solar radiation reaches the tropics than the poles. This uneven heating of the Earth's surface drives the Earth's weather systems.

9   The oceans are a very important component of the climate system.

'The whole of science is nothing more than a refinement of everyday thinking.'
Albert Einstein

4 Energy losses and the energy balance

In Chapter 3 we looked at the amount of energy from the Sun that is intercepted by the Earth and how this varies with both latitude and time. In this chapter we shall examine in more detail what happens to that energy at the Earth's surface and in the atmosphere. In Section 3.1 we considered that for the Earth to be in energy balance the energy received must be matched by the energy lost. Later in this chapter we shall see how the energy balance affects the GMST, but first we look at how energy is redistributed by the atmosphere and how energy is lost.

4.1 Energy loss from the Earth's surface

There are three major ways in which the Earth's surface loses energy: one is the emission of radiation by the surface, and the other two depend on a process called convection occurring in the atmosphere.

4.1.1 Convection

Convection carries energy away from the Earth's surface through currents of air rising upwards. However, it helps to look at this process first in the simpler case of liquids.

Consider a pan of water at room temperature standing over a heat source (e.g. an electric hot plate or a flame) that initially is turned off. There is no upward or downward motion in the water, and the temperature of the water is the same throughout its volume.

If we now turn on the heat source, the base of the pan is heated, which causes a rise in its temperature, and the base of the pan in turn heats the thin layer of water in contact with it, causing the water's temperature to rise. The water in this layer is heated by a process called conduction. This is the transfer of heat from a region of higher temperature (the base of the pan) to a region of lower temperature (the bottom layer of water) because of the direct contact between the two regions. A familiar consequence of conduction is the rising temperature of your hand when you place it against a jug of hot liquid.

The rise in the temperature of the thin layer of water causes it to increase in volume. This is called thermal expansion, a phenomenon displayed by almost all liquids, solids and gases. In fact, it is the phenomenon by which a conventional thermometer works (see Box 2.2).

The expansion of the water as it is heated changes a property of the water called its density. You have probably met this term before. The formal definition of density is the mass of a substance per unit volume, i.e.

$$\text{density} = \frac{\text{mass}}{\text{volume}} \qquad [4.1]$$

The density of a substance depends on both what type of substance it is and whether it is in the form of a solid, liquid or gas.

● What will happen to the density of the thin layer of water when it expands? (Note that its mass is fixed.)

◌ From equation 4.1, if the mass is fixed but the volume increases then overall the quantity on the right of the equation decreases and so the density decreases.

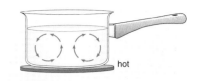

Figure 4.1 A pan of water when it is heated from below, showing convection.

The thin layer of heated water now has a lower density than the cooler water above it and so it will 'float' upwards. In doing so it displaces the overlying cooler, denser water downwards. Figure 4.1 shows a typical pattern of motion. A steady cycle is set up, with warmed water rising to the surface, displacing the cooler water downwards where, in turn, it too is warmed and also rises. Meanwhile, the water that had risen previously has partly cooled, and will then be displaced downwards by hotter rising water. Fluid flow, i.e. the motion of a liquid or gas, driven by temperature-induced density differences is called convection.

Convection occurs in the atmosphere and by this means the Earth's surface loses energy at a considerable rate and the atmosphere gains energy at a corresponding rate. Hot air has a lower density than cool air, so it rises up through the cooler air, transferring heat to it as it does so. Air convection can be seen in the shimmer from the heated air rising from a particularly hot surface such as a paved area in sunlight, or above a central heating radiator or a toaster. We can also see that hot air rises when it is used in hot air balloons (Figure 4.2).

Figure 4.2 The effect of hot air rising is used by balloonists. The burner heats the air enclosed by the balloon to the point where it becomes sufficiently buoyant, i.e. its density becomes sufficiently low, to lift the balloon, the basket and its occupants.

Convection does not happen everywhere at the Earth's surface at all times, but when it does the pattern at any instant at a particular place is typically as shown in Figure 4.3: there are columns of rising air, with much larger regions of descending air between them. This pattern can exist on scales that, at ground level, range from a few centimetres to many metres across. The rising air loses energy to its surroundings and is subsequently displaced downwards. Don't confuse the pattern in Figure 4.3 with the drama of tornadoes. Columns of convection are so gentle that they usually go unnoticed, although glider pilots use them to gain altitude. Glider pilots call them 'thermals'. Some birds also use thermals to enable them to soar to great heights: for example, the American white pelican has been reported to reach an altitude of more than 4000 metres in 10 minutes on a good day, which would be difficult to achieve just by flapping its wings!

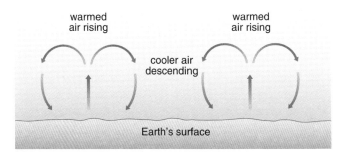

Figure 4.3 Convection transfers energy away from the Earth's surface to the atmosphere. The resulting pattern is known as a convection cell.

4.1.2 Latent heat

In addition to conveying warmed air upwards, convection plays an essential role in a quite different mechanism of energy loss by the Earth's surface: the evaporation of liquid water to produce water vapour. Water, like many substances, can exist in more than one form – solid, liquid or gas – which are called states. The process of converting a substance from a solid to a liquid state (e.g. from ice to water) is called melting, while the reverse process is freezing. Evaporation is the conversion from the liquid to the gaseous state (e.g. from liquid water to water vapour), while condensation is the reverse process. Some substances can be converted directly from the solid to the gaseous state if the conditions are favourable (e.g. from ice to water vapour), a process called sublimation.

● Would you expect sublimation from snow to occur more readily or less readily than evaporation from the oceans?

 First, the rate of evaporation or sublimation depends on the temperature. As oceans are warmer than snow-covered areas, we might expect evaporation from the oceans to occur more readily than sublimation from snow. There is a second reason, which will become clearer in Chapter 5: the particles are held more tightly in a solid than in a liquid, so sublimation requires more energy than evaporation. So, again, we might expect sublimation from snow to occur less readily than evaporation from the oceans, which is indeed the case.

Air is a mixture of various gases (described in Chapter 7), including one particularly important gas – water vapour. Sometimes it is useful to discuss water vapour separately and refer to the rest of the mixture as 'dry air'.

There is a limit to how much water vapour a sample of air can hold. This limit depends on the temperature. If the limit is reached, the air is said to be saturated. Convection is important in evaporation because it carries the water vapour upwards, avoiding saturation of the air at ground level and enabling more water to evaporate from the surface. The source of this surface water is not just oceans and lakes, but any moisture at the surface, such as damp soil and vegetation. Ice can undergo sublimation, which also contributes to the water vapour in the atmosphere.

How do evaporation and sublimation remove energy from the Earth's surface? Both processes require energy to be transferred to the liquid or the ice in order to produce the vapour, even without increasing its temperature. This energy is called latent heat, the word 'latent' denoting that the heat doesn't cause a temperature change but instead causes a change in state, in this case from liquid or solid to gas. To understand latent heat, imagine an ice-cube floating in a glass of water, all at 0 °C. As long as no energy flows into or out of the system, the ice-cube neither melts nor grows in size. If a little energy is now supplied to the system, some of the ice-cube will melt. The temperature does not change because the added energy is all used up to melt some of the ice – the latent heat of melting has been supplied. Only when all the ice has melted will the temperature start to rise. On the other hand, if a little energy is removed from the system, the amount of ice will increase as some of the water freezes. Again the temperature will not change. As energy is removed it is replaced by the latent heat of freezing released as water changes to ice. Only when all the water has turned to ice will the temperature start to fall.

When water evaporates from the Earth's surface, the latent heat is extracted from the Earth and so the surface tends to cool as the water evaporates. Try dampening the palm of your hand with water or perfume and then waving it vigorously to promote evaporation – the cooling should be obvious. The evaporation of sweat in a strong wind also produces obvious cooling. The ways in which the amount of water vapour in the atmosphere is measured are described in Box 4.1.

Box 4.1 Measuring water in the atmosphere

Measures of the amount of water vapour in the atmosphere are known as measures of humidity. There are several different kinds of humidity measurements in meteorology, two of which are summarised below.

The specific humidity is the mass of water vapour, measured in grams, in a kilogram of the dry air and water vapour mixture.

The relative humidity is the ratio of the amount of water vapour contained in a sample of air relative to the amount that it could contain if saturated at the observed dry bulb air temperature, expressed as a percentage.

The term 'dry bulb' temperature needs a little explanation. The temperature measured by a conventional thermometer (Box 2.2) is known as the 'dry bulb temperature'. All temperature readings are assumed to be dry bulb readings unless otherwise specified. The basis for calculating the various measures of humidity is through a combination of dry bulb readings and readings taken using a 'wet bulb thermometer'. This is a thermometer where the reservoir or bulb containing the bulk of the expanding liquid is kept permanently wet. This is usually achieved by surrounding the bulb in a muslin wick dipped in a container of distilled water. The evaporation of water, and the associated energy used in the evaporation process, reduces the temperature of the bulb and so the wet bulb thermometer records a lower temperature than a dry bulb thermometer in the same place and time. The amount of cooling depends on the amount of evaporation, and hence on the degree of saturation, of the surrounding air. The wet bulb thermometer, therefore, indirectly measures humidity.

Readings from wet and dry bulb thermometers provide measurements of humidity at the time the readings are taken but a hygrometer provides a continuous record of humidity. There are several types of hygrometer but a common type uses a sheaf of hair (often human hair) stretched across a metal bar and mechanically linked to a pen. Human hair shrinks by about 2.5% when relative humidity falls from 100% to 0%. As humidity rises the hair stretches again. The stretching and shrinking of the hair moves the pen, which traces out a continuous record of fluctuating humidity over time on a paper strip mounted on a rotating drum.

The temperature of the atmosphere decreases with height (altitude) above ground level. Consequently, as air rises through convection, its temperature decreases. If the temperature falls low enough, some of the vapour in the air condenses to form a large number of liquid droplets or even icy particles – which are visible as clouds. Indeed, puffy clouds often appear in rising columns of air, as Figure 4.4 shows. If it takes an input of heat to produce vapour from liquid or solid, you might expect heat to be given out in the reverse process, i.e. in the condensation of vapour to produce liquid and solid, which indeed is the case. Exactly the same quantity of heat is given out during condensation as was taken in during evaporation, provided the starting and final temperatures are the same. This is a consequence of a fundamental law called the First Law of Thermodynamics, which states that energy can be neither created nor destroyed, only transformed from one form to another. The latent heat given out by condensation heats the atmosphere.

(a)

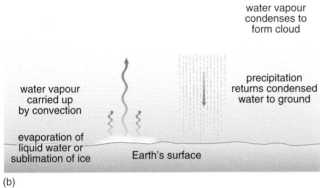

(b)

Figure 4.4 (a) Clouds forming in rising columns of air, a consequence of water vapour carried upwards by convection. (b) Water is evaporated from the Earth's surface, which consequently loses energy through latent heat. When the water vapour condenses, the latent heat is given out and raises the temperature of the atmosphere. Energy is thus transferred from the Earth's surface to the atmosphere. Precipitation from the atmosphere returns water to the ground.

The latent heat extracted from the ground in the evaporation of water, and given out again when the water condenses in the atmosphere, thus transfers energy from the Earth's surface to the Earth's atmosphere.

Ultimately, the condensed water returns to the ground as precipitation, mostly as rain or snow, where it is susceptible again to evaporation or sublimation as the cycle repeats itself. (We shall discuss this water cycle in more detail in Chapter 5.) So, this movement of water from the surface of the Earth into the atmosphere and back again acts like a conveyor belt for the transfer of energy from the surface to the atmosphere.

This process depends on convection and wind. If there is no convection and no wind, the water vapour in the layer of air next to the ground is not carried away. It therefore becomes saturated (i.e. it cannot hold any more water vapour) and further evaporation stops. In this case, the only latent heat extracted from the ground is for the initial evaporation. Conduction, which you might think is an alternative means of transferring energy upwards, is in fact very ineffective.

● A global map of mean daily precipitation for June, July and August is shown in Figure 4.5. Can you explain the pattern of precipitation between 30° N and 30° S in terms of convection and comment on the latent heat energy transfers associated with this pattern?

◉ The most intense rainfall band is located close to the Equator, largely just north of 0° because it is in the northern summer (June, July and August). This suggests that the high amounts of heat received generate powerful convection systems carrying evaporated water vapour high into the atmosphere where cooling and condensation produce intense rainfall. Energy is required to evaporate the moisture from the Earth's surface so latent heat is transferred from the ground to the air. As the rising air cools, latent heat is given up as the moisture condenses, so heating the atmosphere.

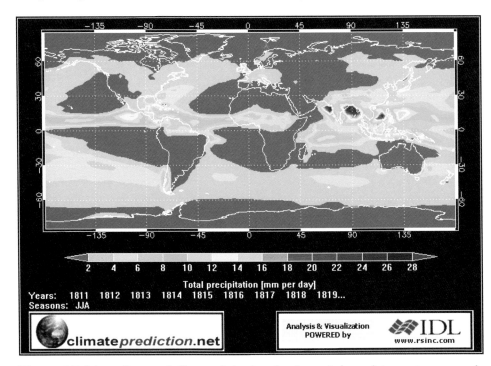

Figure 4.5 Map of mean daily precipitation for June, July and August, averaged over several years.

Although the land is warmer than the ocean, the ocean is the primary source of evaporated moisture, so the precipitation tends to be most intense and widespread over, or near to, the oceans (see Figure 1.3). There is a disruption to this simple pattern over Asia, in particular near India and Tibet. We shall examine the causes of this in more detail in Chapter 6.

4.1.3 Infrared radiation emitted by the Earth's surface

Although convection is an important means by which the Earth's surface loses energy, the greatest rate of energy loss is by electromagnetic radiation *emitted* by the Earth's surface. This emitted radiation is not the same as the solar radiation *reflected* by the Earth's surface, which was shown in Figure 3.8c. Reflected radiation merely 'bounces' off the surface, whereas emitted radiation originates within the surface. What is the source of this emitted radiation?

In everyday life we see most objects by *reflected* radiation. During the day we see outdoor scenes by the visible solar radiation (sunlight) they reflect, and during the night we see indoor scenes by the light they reflect that originates from a source such as an electric light bulb. The sources of this reflected radiation are the Sun and the bulb, respectively. If we look at the glowing bulb itself we are seeing the light emitted by the hot wire in it: this wire is emitting light, not reflecting it from elsewhere. Likewise, if we could look directly at the Sun (please don't – it will damage your eyes!) then we would see the light emitted by the Sun.

The emitted radiation originates from the atoms that constitute the objects. (You will learn about atoms in Chapter 7.) Atoms are always jostling about, and one consequence of this is that they emit electromagnetic radiation. The details of the process are not relevant here: the important point is that *all* objects emit electromagnetic radiation – this includes you, the surface of the Earth and the atmosphere.

Why then can we see the emission from the bulb and the Sun but not that from the Earth's surface? The answer is that the Sun and the bulb emit sufficient visible radiation which our eyes can see, whereas the Earth's surface emits negligible amounts of visible radiation. The radiation emitted by the Earth's surface is largely infrared wavelengths, which are not visible to the human eye (see Figure 3.4). Figure 4.6 shows a graph of the power of the radiation versus wavelength – this is called a spectrum.

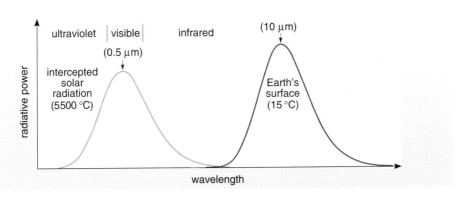

Figure 4.6 The distribution over wavelength of the power of the radiation emitted by the Earth's surface, and of the solar radiation that the Earth intercepts. The values of the wavelengths (see Box 3.2) corresponding to the peak of each spectrum are indicated. Both spectra have been simplified. The approximate temperatures of the Sun and the Earth's surface are also indicated.

The curve labelled 'Earth's surface' in Figure 4.6 shows how the power of the radiation from the Earth's surface is distributed among the various wavelengths. (Remember from Chapter 3 that power is the same as energy per unit of time.)

- From Figure 4.6, which sub-range of electromagnetic radiation is emitted by the Earth's surface, and which sub-ranges are absent?

- The Earth's surface emits infrared radiation but it does not emit appreciable amounts of visible or ultraviolet radiation.

Figure 4.6 also shows the spectrum of the solar radiation intercepted by the Earth. You can see that this spectrum is dominated by shorter wavelengths and the maximum power – the 'peak' – is at visible wavelengths.

But why are the wavelength ranges different? It all comes down to temperature. The GMST is 15 °C whereas the surface of the Sun is at the huge temperature of over 5500 °C. The higher the temperature of an object, the more the spectrum of emitted radiation shifts to shorter wavelengths. This is why a metal heated to a modest temperature glows red, whereas at a higher temperature it glows yellow – yellow light has a shorter wavelength than red light (see Figure 3.4).

Another property of emitted radiation that changes with temperature is its total power. Figure 4.7 compares the spectrum of the radiation emitted by the Earth's surface at its present mean temperature of 15 °C with the spectrum if the surface temperature was 50 °C. You can see that, when the temperature rises, as well as a shift to shorter wavelengths there is also a general increase in the power radiated. This is an extremely important result, crucial for our understanding of the GMST, as the next question shows.

- In applying the leaky tank analogy to the GMST, we asserted that as the GMST rises, the rate of energy loss from the Earth's surface increases. In one or two sentences, explain why Figure 4.7 supports this assertion.

- Figure 4.7 shows that the higher the GMST, the greater the rate at which the Earth's surface emits radiation (the higher the radiative power). This supports the assertion that, as the GMST rises, the rate of energy loss from the Earth's surface increases.

Finally, there is an apparently curious feature of Figures 4.6 and 4.7 that needs explaining. In Figure 4.7 a rise in temperature from 15 °C to 50 °C produces a substantial increase in the power of the radiation, whereas in Figure 4.6 a much larger difference in temperature of 15 °C to 5500 °C is associated with a rather slight difference in power. This is because in Figure 4.6 the solar spectrum is for the solar radiation intercepted by the Earth, as in Figures 3.6 and 3.11. This is only a tiny fraction of the power emitted by the Sun. By contrast, in Figure 4.7 the radiation in both cases is from the same object: the whole surface of the Earth.

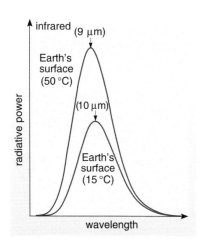

Figure 4.7 The spectrum of the radiation emitted by the Earth's surface at temperatures of 15 °C and 50 °C.

4.2 Atmospheric radiation absorbed by the Earth's surface

You have seen that the Earth's surface is at a temperature such that most of the emitted radiation is at infrared wavelengths. Some of the emitted radiation escapes to space, but most of it is absorbed by the Earth's atmosphere. This absorbed radiation is a fourth source of energy for the atmosphere.

- What are the three sources you have already met?

◉ There is absorbed solar radiation (see Figure 3.10), energy transferred by convection, and latent heat given out when water vapour condenses.

The energy gains by the atmosphere sustain the atmospheric temperatures. The atmosphere is far less dense than the Earth but it still consists of matter and therefore it too emits radiation characteristic of its temperature. Atmospheric temperatures are not hugely different from surface temperatures, and so the radiation emitted by the atmosphere is also predominantly at infrared wavelengths. This atmospheric radiation gives rise to a second source of energy for the surface.

- What is the only significant source of energy for the Earth's surface that has been described so far?

◉ This is the solar radiation absorbed by the Earth's surface (Figure 3.10).

Atmospheric radiation travels in all directions, and some of it escapes to space. The rest ultimately reaches the ground, and thus constitutes another energy gain by the surface, to add to solar radiation. However, it is important to realise that atmospheric radiation is derived from solar radiation. This is because all of the four energy gains by the atmosphere depend on solar radiation. The atmosphere is warmed by the Sun directly; it is also warmed indirectly by convection, latent heat and surface emission of radiation, all of which arise from the heating of the Earth's surface by solar radiation. Therefore, the energy gain by the Earth's surface is dominated by solar radiation, whether it is direct or indirect.

Figure 4.8 brings together the various processes that we have considered in this section and in Section 4.1. As in Figure 3.10, the width of each arrow is proportional to the rate of energy transfer. The upward-pointing arrow on the left

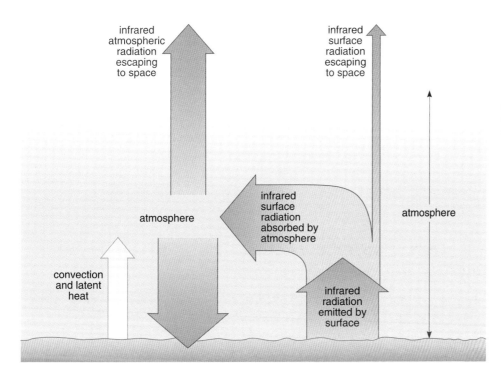

Figure 4.8 The exchanges of infrared radiation involving the Earth's surface and atmosphere, including the convective and latent heat transfers. The width of each arrow is proportional to the rate of energy transfer. Values are added in Figure 4.9.

represents the rate at which energy is transferred from the Earth's surface to the atmosphere through convection plus latent heat. The arrow on the right leaving the Earth's surface represents the rate at which infrared radiation is emitted by the Earth's surface. This arrow splits into two: a thin arrow representing the small amount of emitted radiation that escapes to space, and a thicker arrow that curves and ends in the atmosphere.

● What does this curved arrow represent?

◉ It represents the rate at which radiation emitted by the Earth's surface is absorbed by the atmosphere.

The central arrows originate in the atmosphere, and represent the infrared radiation emitted by the atmosphere. The upward-pointing arrow represents the amount of this infrared radiation that escapes to space, and the downward-pointing arrow represents the amount that is absorbed by the Earth's surface. Note that even though the arrows starting and stopping in the atmosphere do so in a small region in the centre of Figure 4.8, the atmospheric energy gains and losses take place throughout the atmosphere.

We have now met all of the important energy gains and losses at the Earth's surface. The time has come to bring them together and get an overview, so that we can see the processes that determine the GMST.

Figure 4.9 Rates of energy gain and loss by the Earth's surface and atmosphere. The width of each arrow is proportional to the rate of energy transfer and 100 units represent the rate at which solar radiation is intercepted by the Earth.

4.3 What determines the GMST?

4.3.1 Overall energy gains and losses

Figure 4.9 is what we have been working towards: a diagram giving an overview of the rates of energy gain and loss by the Earth's surface and atmosphere.

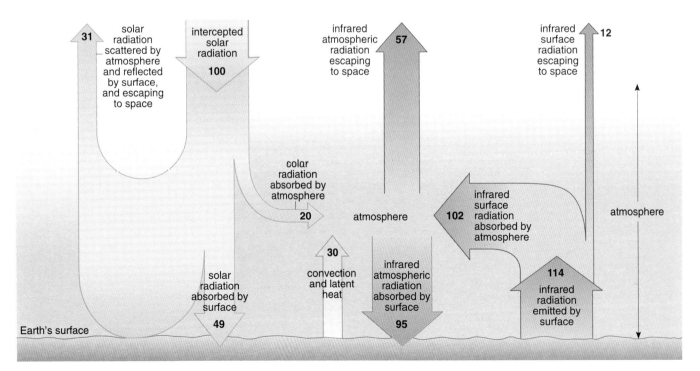

The component parts of this diagram are Figures 3.10 and 4.8, which have already been discussed, but we shall now explore this synthesis in some detail.

The left-hand side of Figure 4.9 is the same as Figure 3.10: it shows the rates of energy gain and loss by the Earth's surface and atmosphere that involve solar radiation directly. Remember that 100 units represent the rate at which solar electromagnetic radiation is intercepted by the Earth: of these 100 units, 49 units are absorbed by the surface and 20 units by the atmosphere, and the remaining 31 units escape back to space.

The central part of Figure 4.9 (coloured green) shows the rate of energy transfer from the Earth's surface to the atmosphere by a combination of convection and latent heat. There are 30 units transferred in this way, and it is a loss from the surface.

The right-hand side of Figure 4.9 is exactly the same as Figure 4.8 and involves the infrared radiation described in Section 4.2, but now values have been added to the arrows. If you start at the extreme right, you can see that 114 units are emitted by the Earth's surface, with 12 of the 114 units escaping to space, and the major part – 102 units – being absorbed by the atmosphere. The atmosphere emits infrared radiation at a rate of 152 units. Of this, 57 units escape to space, and the remaining 95 units are absorbed by the surface.

At this point, a question might spring to mind: if the Earth intercepts solar radiation at the rate of 100 units, how can 114 units be emitted by the Earth's surface, and 152 units be emitted by the atmosphere? Tackling the following question should help you understand this apparent paradox.

● From Figure 4.9 calculate the difference between the rate of energy gain and the rate of energy loss for:

(i) the Earth as a whole (consider the solar radiation intercepted by the Earth, and the radiation returning or escaping to space from the atmosphere and the surface)

(ii) the Earth's surface

(iii) the Earth's atmosphere.

(i) For the Earth as a whole, the total rate of energy gain (solar radiation intercepted) is 100 units, and the total rate of loss is the sum of the upward-pointing arrows at the top of the atmosphere. This is 31 units + 57 units + 12 units = 100 units – a difference of zero.

(ii) The total rate of energy gain by the Earth's surface is the sum of the downward-pointing arrows that penetrate down to the Earth's surface in Figure 4.9. This is 49 units + 95 units = 144 units. The total rate of loss is the sum of the upward-pointing arrows originating at the Earth's surface: 30 units + 114 units = 144 units. Again the difference is zero.

(iii) Proceeding as in (ii), the total rate of energy gain by the atmosphere is 20 units + 30 units + 102 units = 152 units, and the total rate of loss is 95 units + 57 units = 152 units. Again the difference is zero.

● From your calculations above, what can you conclude about the GMST?

◉ From (ii) above, at the Earth's surface the rate of energy gain equals the rate of loss. The surface is therefore in a steady state and the GMST is not changing.

The answer to (i) above shows that there is no net energy gain or loss by the Earth, and the answers to parts (ii) and (iii) show that this is also the case separately for the surface and the atmosphere. Everything is in a dynamic steady state: in spite of all those energy flows there is no net accumulation of energy in any part of the system, and no net loss. Perhaps it is now less puzzling that some of the rates of energy exchange in Figure 4.9 exceed the rate at which solar energy is intercepted by the Earth. The rates of energy exchange between different parts of a system in a steady state can be as high as you like, as long as the rate of energy gain by each part equals the rate of energy loss by the same part, so the net energy transfer is zero. In other words, the rates of circulation of energy within a system can be greater than the rate of flow into and out of a system.

Now let's take a closer look at the radiation balance of the Earth–atmosphere system, to understand how the picture varies with latitude. The solid curve in Figure 4.10 shows how the average amount of solar radiation absorbed by the Earth and its atmosphere varies with latitude. Much of this incoming solar radiation is visible-wavelength radiation (Figure 4.6). A proportion of this energy is then re-radiated, at longer infrared wavelengths (see Box 3.2), although little is radiated directly into space – as we have seen, most is absorbed in the atmosphere. The atmosphere is therefore heated from below and itself re-emits longwave radiation into space, mostly from the top of the cloud cover. As temperatures at the top of the cloud cover do not vary much with latitude, neither does the intensity of longwave radiation emitted to space: this is shown by the dashed curve in Figure 4.10.

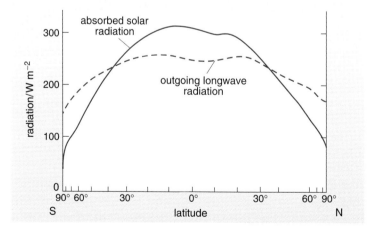

Figure 4.10 Variation with latitude of the solar radiation absorbed by the Earth–atmosphere system (solid curve) and the outgoing longwave radiation lost to space (dashed curve). Values are averaged over the year, and are scaled according to the area of the Earth's surface in different latitude bands.

● Suggest two reasons why the curve for the absorbed solar radiation in Figure 4.10 has the general shape it does. (Hint: refer to Table 3.1.)

The main and most obvious reason is that more solar radiation reaches the Earth's surface at low latitudes than at high, for reasons demonstrated by Figure 3.11b. The second reason is that, of the solar radiation that reaches the Earth's surface, much more is reflected at high latitudes than low, particularly because of the high albedo values of ice and snow (Table 3.1).

● Over which latitudes does the Earth–atmosphere system have a net gain of radiation and over which does it have a net loss?

The Earth–atmosphere system has a net gain of radiation between about 40° S and 35° N where the levels of absorbed solar radiation (solid line on Figure 4.10) are higher than the outgoing longwave radiation (dashed line); poleward of those latitudes, there is a net loss of radiation.

Note that together the two regions in Figure 4.10 that show a 'net loss' are compensated by the region in the centre where there is a 'net gain'. This demonstrates that, at least over short time-scales, the overall Earth–atmosphere radiation budget is in balance, so the Earth is neither cooling down nor heating up. Whether this is true over time-scales of decades is, of course, at the heart of modelling climate change.

Rather than considering flows of energy at the Earth's surface, we could consider the balance between incoming and outgoing energy for the atmosphere–ocean–land system as a whole, i.e. at the 'top of the atmosphere'. This approach is much simpler in one crucial respect: radiation is the only energy transport mechanism that matters.

The only way in which the Earth as a whole receives energy from the Sun is in the form of shortwave (mostly visible) radiation, and the only way it emits it back out into space is in the form of longwave (mostly infrared) radiation.

● Why don't convection and release of latent heat occur beyond the top of the atmosphere?

Space is a vacuum, so there is no medium (air) in which convection and release of latent heat can occur.

Satellite monitoring now allows us to measure the incoming and outgoing radiation over the entire surface of the Earth. Figure 4.11 shows both the reflected shortwave radiation and the emitted longwave radiation during March 2000.

● Do Figures 4.10 and 4.11 present consistent pictures of the latitude-dependence of outgoing longwave radiation?

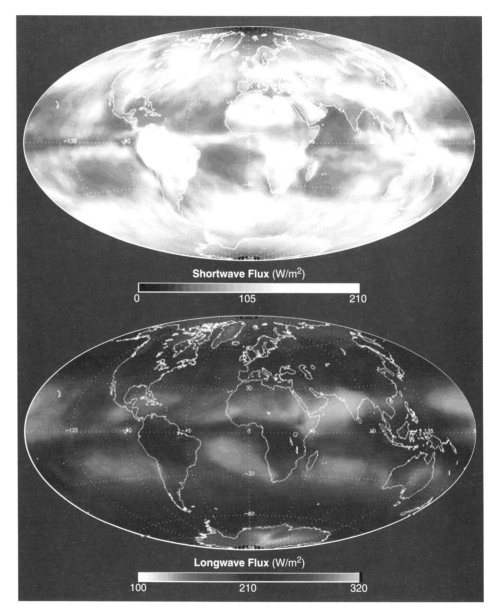

Figure 4.11 Images of the Earth's climate system during March 2000. The upper image shows shortwave radiation (flux), i.e. sunlight, which is reflected back into space by the Earth, averaged over the entire month, and the lower image shows longwave radiation, which is emitted by the Earth back into space.

⊘ The lower part of Figure 4.11 shows that between 45° N and 45° S the Earth radiates in the range of about 220 to 320 W m^{-2}, but radiates less, at about 150 to 200 W m^{-2}, closer to the poles. This is consistent with the averaged values shown by the dashed line in Figure 4.10.

Despite the positive radiation balance at low latitudes and the negative one at high latitudes, there is no evidence that low-latitude regions are steadily heating up while high-latitude regions are steadily cooling. The reason for this, of course, is the continual redistribution of heat over the globe by winds in the atmosphere and currents in the ocean – we shall examine this in Chapter 5. Before then, however, we shall continue our discussion of the way the energy balance determines the GMST.

4.3.2 Why the GMST has a particular value

In broad terms, we can see from Figure 4.9 that the value of the GMST depends on the following factors.

- The rate at which the Earth intercepts solar radiation: this rate is obtained by multiplying the area over which radiation is intercepted (the area of the disc in Figures 3.6 and 3.11) by the solar constant.

- The properties of the atmosphere, particularly those that influence:
  - the scattering and absorption of solar radiation
  - the absorption of the (infrared) radiation emitted by the Earth's surface
  - the emission of (infrared) radiation by the atmosphere
  - the rate of energy transfer via convection and latent heat.

- The properties of the Earth's surface, particularly those that influence:
  - the reflection and absorption of solar radiation
  - the emission of radiation by the surface (which is at infrared wavelengths)
  - the availability of water for evaporation.

If any of these factors is changed, the GMST will change, unless, in changing several factors at once, there is overall compensation, in which case there is no net effect on the GMST.

Let's examine the case of the solar constant and carry out a 'thought experiment'. Suppose that initially there is a steady state with the Sun shining as it is today, when suddenly, as in Figure 4.12a, the solar constant increases to a slightly higher value, with no change in atmospheric and surface properties. What would happen? At once, the Earth's surface would receive more solar radiation than before, and because the surface would absorb the same fraction of the radiation it would therefore absorb more solar radiation. At the instant that the solar constant changed there would be no change in the rate of energy loss by the surface, so the GMST would start to rise, as in Figure 4.12b. This rise in GMST would cause the surface to emit more infrared radiation (Figure 4.7) and so the rate of energy loss would increase as the temperature increased, as in Figure 4.12c. The GMST would continue to rise until the rate at which energy was lost by the Earth equalled the new rate of energy gain. There would then be a new steady state, with the GMST higher than before.

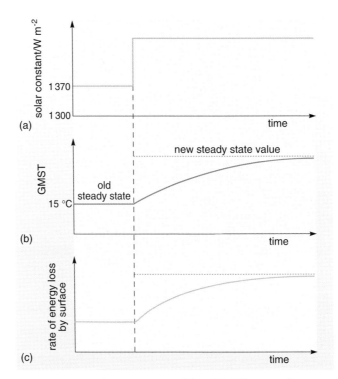

Figure 4.12 The response of the GMST to an increase in the solar constant (a and b), and the consequent increase in the rate of energy loss from the Earth (c). Note that the vertical axis in (a) does not start at zero, so the solar constant is increased only slightly.

As we showed in Sections 3.4 and 3.5, the solar constant does indeed vary, by about 0.1% over a decade or so and by rather more in the longer term, because of changes in the solar luminosity and the eccentricity of the Earth's orbit. The steady state in Figure 4.9 is therefore slightly disturbed in reality and, consequently, the GMST does vary.

Changes in incoming solar radiation such as those described above, or any other factor that has the potential to cause changes in the Earth's climate system, is known as a forcing mechanism. In general, you can think of a forcing mechanism as something that forces a system to respond in a way other than it would do if left alone. In the context of modelling climate, a 'forcing mechanism' often means something that affects the radiation balance of the Earth, either locally or globally.

Climate modellers describe the size of the response of the climate system to a forcing of given magnitude as the climate's sensitivity. Unfortunately, the Earth's sensitivity to climate forcing is hard to measure or predict. Theoretical modelling suggests that an increase in the average amount of incoming solar flux of 4.0 to 4.5 W m^{-2} (the present day average is 343 W m^{-2}, Figure 3.11) could cause a change in temperature of anything from 1.5 to 5.5 °C, which means that the climate's sensitivity is of the order of 0.5 to 1.0 °C for 1 W m^{-2}, say 0.75 °C per W m^{-2} of forcing. (Note that these figures are given as round numbers; the sensitivity to change is not known sufficiently accurately to justify writing them more precisely. We shall return to this in Chapter 8.)

Notice the uncertainty in the estimate. One reason for this is the time it takes for the Earth to respond to a change: its systems have huge inertia. If the solar flux were to be completely extinguished for a few minutes, as it is locally during a solar eclipse, the effects would be negligible. However, if the solar flux were to decrease abruptly and permanently by 0.1%, this would ultimately show up in small changes in all aspects of the climate system – the temperature distribution within the atmosphere and oceans, the extents of polar ice-caps and of tropical rainforests, and so on. Each of these changes would have its own effects – so it would take a long time, perhaps a century, before the climate system settled into a new equilibrium. Thus, in trying to assess the sensitivity of the Earth's climate to changes in forcing, we have to take into account all of the various processes that may come into play, and their characteristic time-scales. An important implication of this is that the climate system will not have the same sensitivity to different types of climate forcing. To appreciate radiation balances fully, we need to know more about energy and the atmosphere and this topic is explored more fully in Chapter 5.

To conclude this chapter we shall consider one particularly important factor that affects the GMST: the effect of changing the rate at which the atmosphere absorbs and emits infrared radiation, which brings us to the much-publicised greenhouse effect.

4.3.3 The greenhouse effect

In order to discuss the greenhouse effect, it is convenient to distinguish in Figure 4.9 between the radiation emitted by the Earth's surface and the radiation emitted by the Sun.

● Which of these two types of radiation is characterised by longer wavelengths?

○ The radiation emitted from the Earth's surface, which is principally infrared (see Figure 4.6).

Moreover, the radiation from the Earth's surface is confined to the longer wavelength part of the infrared sub-range of the spectrum, whereas the solar radiation in the infrared sub-range is at shorter wavelengths. Consequently, the radiation from the Earth's surface is often called longwave infrared radiation. The atmosphere also emits longwave infrared radiation.

● From Figure 4.9, write down the fraction of the radiation emitted by the Earth's surface that is absorbed by the atmosphere. Express the fraction in decimal form and as a percentage.

◉ The fraction is $\frac{102}{114}$ = 0.89, which as a percentage is 0.89 × 100 = 89%.

Thus, most of the radiation emitted by the Earth's surface is absorbed by the atmosphere. By contrast, only 20% of the incoming solar radiation is absorbed by the atmosphere. The fractions (or percentages) absorbed are called the absorptivities.

Suppose that, somehow, the atmospheric properties were suddenly adjusted so that the only change was a reduction in longwave infrared absorptivity (see Figure 4.13a): suppose that all other atmospheric properties, the solar constant, and all the surface properties remain the same. The atmosphere would therefore absorb a smaller proportion of the infrared radiation emitted by the surface. In Figure 4.9, of the 114 units of energy emitted by the Earth's surface the amount absorbed by the atmosphere would be less than 102 units and the amount escaping to space would be correspondingly more. It turns out that the atmosphere would then emit less infrared radiation. This means that there would be less radiation from the atmosphere for the Earth's surface to absorb: it would absorb less than the 95 units in Figure 4.9. Nothing else has changed at the surface, so the Earth's surface would be losing energy faster than it would be gaining it.

● So, what would happen to the surface temperature?

◉ It would fall – the surface would cool.

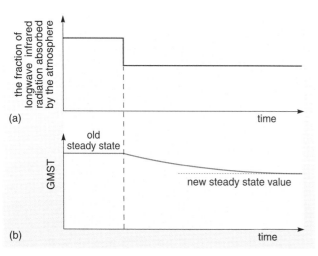

(a)

(b)

Figure 4.13 When the atmospheric absorptivity of longwave infrared radiation is reduced (a), the GMST decreases in response (b), all else remaining the same.

However, the cooling would not continue indefinitely. The cooler the surface, the lower the rate at which it emits radiation. It is also possible that the rate of energy loss via convection and latent heat would fall. The cooling of the surface would thus continue until the rate of energy loss by the surface equals the new, lower rate of gain. A new steady state is then in place, with the surface at a new, lower temperature, as in Figure 4.13b.

● Now work through what would happen if the atmospheric properties were suddenly adjusted so that the only change was an *increase* in longwave infrared absorptivity.

◉ The atmosphere would absorb a larger proportion of the infrared radiation emitted by the surface. In Figure 4.9 the 114 units of energy emitted by the Earth's surface would divide into more than 102 units absorbed by the atmosphere and less than 12 units escaping to space. The atmosphere has to get rid of this additional energy relatively rapidly, because its ability to store energy is very limited (air has a low heat capacity – see Section 3.2.2). So, to balance its own 'energy budget', the atmosphere has to emit more infrared radiation. This means that there would be more radiation for the Earth's surface to absorb: it would absorb more than the 95 units in Figure 4.9. Nothing else has changed at the surface, so the Earth's surface would be gaining energy faster than it would be losing it and the surface temperature would increase. The warming would not, however, continue indefinitely. The warmer the surface, the faster the rate at which it emits radiation. (The rate of energy loss through convection and latent heat would probably increase as well.) The warming of the surface thus continues until the rate of energy loss by the surface equals the new, higher rate of energy gain. A new steady state is then reached, with the surface at a new, higher temperature.

For the Earth today, if there were no radiation emitted by the atmosphere, and if all else stayed the same, the GMST would be about −20 °C. Life on Earth would be very different, and perhaps there would be no life here at all. The atmosphere thus acts as a powerful 'radiation trap', and the GMST is considerably higher as a consequence. The rise in surface temperature that results from the radiation emitted by the atmosphere is called the greenhouse effect.

The greenhouse effect gets its name from the higher temperature reached in daylight in an unheated greenhouse than in the air outside. This arises in two ways. First, containment of warm air that would otherwise convect upwards and be replaced by cooler air, reduces loss of heat by convection. Second, a small part of the difference is because the glass panes in a greenhouse behave towards radiation rather like the Earth's atmosphere does (Figure 4.14). The panes absorb a large fraction of the longwave infrared radiation emitted by the plants, soil and other surfaces within the greenhouse. Some of this radiation is then emitted back into the greenhouse by the panes to make a small additional contribution to the rise in temperature in the greenhouse. As you read on, you will realise that this latter, *minor* reason for greenhouses warming up in the daylight is analogous to the *major* mechanism of the so-called greenhouse effect in the atmosphere.

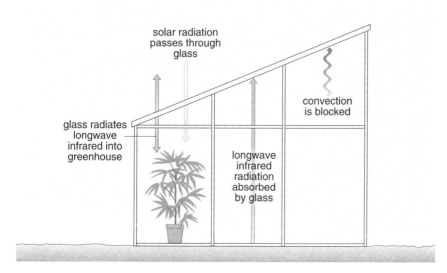

Figure 4.14 How a greenhouse can be warmer than the surrounding air.

For the Earth, the fact that the GMST is considerably higher than it would be if the atmosphere allowed longwave infrared radiation to escape to space shows that the greenhouse effect is not a 'bad thing': indeed, it is a 'good thing'! It is changes in the greenhouse effect that could have undesirable consequences for humans, by causing changes in the GMST, which would in turn cause changes in the climate, the weather, the crops that could grow in each region, and so on. The greenhouse effect depends on atmospheric gases that strongly absorb longwave infrared radiation. These are called greenhouse gases. The greater the amount of greenhouse gas in the atmosphere, the higher the GMST (if everything else stays the same).

In Chapter 7 we shall look in more detail at the chemistry of the atmosphere and see which gases are primarily responsible for the greenhouse effect. First, however, in Chapters 5 and 6 we shall look at the large-scale structure and movement of the atmosphere.

4.4 Summary of Chapter 4

1   Heat is transported from the Earth's surface to the atmosphere by three processes: by convection in the atmosphere; by the absorption of latent heat in evaporation from the ground and by its release in the condensation of water in the atmosphere; and by longwave infrared radiation.

2   Most of the longwave infrared radiation emitted by the Earth's surface is absorbed by the atmosphere. This, plus the convective and latent heat transfers, sustains the atmospheric temperature, and therefore sustains the rate at which the atmosphere emits infrared radiation.

3   The GMST depends on the rate at which the Earth's surface gains energy, and the rate at which it loses energy. If the two rates are equal then there is a steady state and the GMST does not change. If the rates are unequal then the GMST will change. The rate of loss of energy from the Earth's surface increases as the GMST rises. It is difficult to model the sensitivity of the GMST to forcing mechanisms.

4   The greenhouse effect is the process whereby the atmosphere absorbs much of the longwave radiation emitted by the Earth and re-radiates it, some back in the direction of the Earth's surface. Without a greenhouse effect, the GMST would be about -20 °C.

5 The Earth's atmosphere: structure and water content

'Space isn't remote at all. It's only an hour's drive away if your car could go straight upwards.'
Fred Hoyle

The Earth is surrounded by a relatively thin layer of a mixture of gases that we call 'air', and the complete layer of air is known as the atmosphere. To see just how thin the atmosphere is in relation to the size of the Earth look at Figure 5.1, where the atmosphere appears as a thin blue band following the Earth's curvature. In Chapters 3 and 4 you saw how the global mean surface temperature (GMST) depends on the energy balance at the Earth's surface and how the presence of an atmosphere has a major effect on this energy balance. The ultimate source of the energy is the Sun, but solar radiation is not simply absorbed by the Earth's surface, and the radiation emitted by the surface does not simply escape to space.

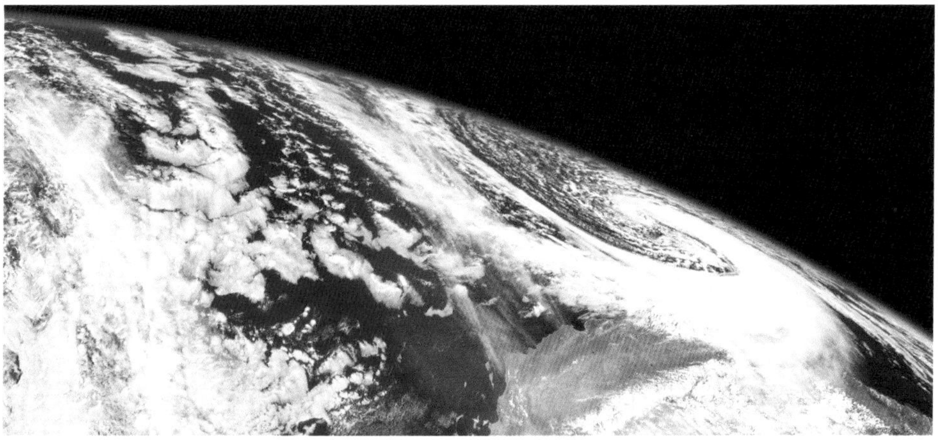

Figure 5.1 View from a satellite, looking northwest over the Pacific Ocean, showing a low-pressure weather system off the coast of California.

- Can you recall four ways in which the Earth's atmosphere affects the GMST?
- The atmosphere:

  (i) reduces the amount of solar radiation that reaches the surface

  (ii) absorbs some of the infrared radiation emitted by the surface

  (iii) emits infrared radiation, some of which is absorbed by the surface

  (iv) enables energy to be lost from the surface through convection and latent heat transfer.

To appreciate the factors that control these processes, we need to understand the structure, movement and composition of the atmosphere. This is the main aim of this chapter and Chapters 6 and 7, but it is not the only aim. Our examination of the atmosphere is also an opportunity to demonstrate that, although its behaviour is complex, it depends on some basic scientific principles.

As noted above, the atmosphere consists largely of a mixture of gases. In Section 5.1 we start by examining exactly what the term 'gas' means, and how some of its properties can be explained and predicted. We apply these ideas to the atmosphere in Section 5.2, to help you understand the vertical structure of the atmosphere, in particular why air pressure decreases with height. In Sections 5.3 and 5.4 we consider the various forms in which water exists in the atmosphere, and how it is cycled between the atmosphere and the ground. From this we shall begin to see the many ways in which water plays a major role in determining the Earth's current and future climate.

5.1   What is a gas?

5.1.1   Gas as a state of matter

One of the key properties of the atoms and molecules (we shall call them 'particles' for simplicity) that make up all matter is that they are attracted to each other, but this attraction decreases the farther apart they are. The distance between particles depends on whether they are in a solid, liquid or gaseous form. In the solid state, the particles are packed closely such that their mutual attraction holds them tightly together. As a result the particles have fixed positions relative to each other, as shown in Figure 5.2a: the particles do not swap places but they 'vibrate' about their fixed positions, as Figure 5.2a shows for a few of them. One of the properties of a solid is that it keeps its shape irrespective of the shape of its container: that is, it does not flow. In the liquid state, the particles are still close enough to be attracted to each other but they are not arranged in a regular way (Figure 5.2b). The particles move around, jostling and swapping positions. As a liquid flows, it takes up the shape of the vessel it is in. In the gaseous state, the particles are so much further apart that there is little attraction between them (Figure 5.2c). In this state the particles move around rapidly in a random, chaotic manner, frequently colliding with, and bouncing off, each other and the walls of the container. A gas will fill its container completely, whatever the volume or shape.

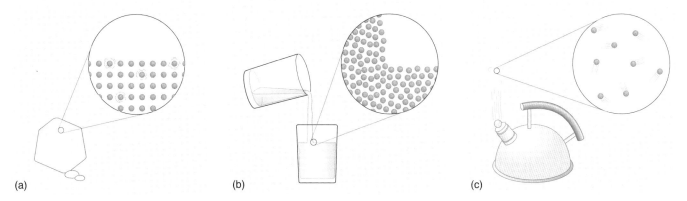

(a)   (b)   (c)

Figure 5.2   The arrangement of particles in (a) the solid, (b) the liquid and (c) the gaseous state. (Note that the steam from a kettle is usually a mixture of the true gaseous state of water, i.e. water vapour, and fine droplets of liquid water.)

● In Section 4.1, we used the definition of density (mass/volume) to argue that thermal expansion will reduce the density of the air. Is this conclusion consistent with the above description of a gas?

◉ Yes. If the volume of a fixed mass of gas increases, there will be fewer particles and hence less mass in a specified volume, so the density decreases.

Water is an example of a material that can exist in different states, as discussed in Section 4.1.2. Below its freezing temperature (0 °C) it exists as a solid – ice. When it melts, it is a liquid. When this liquid evaporates, either gently at temperatures between 0 °C and 100 °C or more vigorously when it boils at 100 °C, water becomes a gas referred to as water vapour. We can explain these changes of state in terms of particles. When a solid melts, the ordered positioning of the particles starts to break down. Melting occurs at a particular temperature, known as the melting temperature or melting point, and involves the transition from a state where the particles don't swap positions, to one where they do. This transition requires an input of energy, so that the vibrating particles have enough energy to overcome the forces of attraction between them and move from their fixed positions. Thus, to melt a solid at its melting temperature we need to put energy into the material. This is the latent heat, which you met in Section 4.1.2. Now you can see that this arises because the arrangement of the particles must change. Freezing is the opposite process to melting: a liquid changes into a solid. The freezing temperature is the same as the melting temperature, so a substance can exist as either solid or liquid at this temperature, depending on how much latent heat has been added or extracted.

● What happens to the particles in a liquid during freezing?

◉ Freezing of a liquid involves the transition from a state in which the particles can swap positions (the liquid state) to one in which the particles occupy specific positions (the solid state).

Evaporation of a liquid to a gas involves a transition from a state in which the particles are close together to one in which they are much further apart. In this transition, energy needs to be supplied to overcome the mutual attraction between the particles and cause them to spread apart. Thus we need to provide energy to convert a substance from a liquid into a gas, as you saw in Section 4.1.2. This energy is called the latent heat of vaporisation. Section 4.1.2 noted that this is why our skin cools when water evaporates from it: our skin supplies the energy for the water to evaporate and so is cooled down.

Evaporation usually occurs from the surface of a liquid, as shown in Figure 5.3. It can occur at any temperature. However, the ease with which particles move from the liquid to the gaseous state increases as the temperature of the liquid increases. This is one of the reasons why washing dries quickly on a hot summer day. The highest temperature at which a liquid exists is called its boiling temperature or boiling point. At this temperature the conversion of the liquid into a gas occurs so readily that gas bubbles form in the liquid and erupt from its surface, which is how we recognise boiling. At higher temperatures the substance is completely gaseous. Condensation is the reverse transition from the gaseous state to the liquid state.

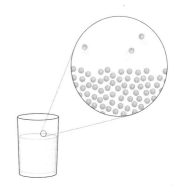

Figure 5.3   When a liquid evaporates, particles leave the surface of the liquid.

● Describe the process of condensation at the particle level.

◉ Condensation involves the transition from a state in which the particles are far away from, and effectively independent of, each other to a state in which the particles are closer together and the attraction between them is greater.

For evaporation to occur, an input of energy – latent heat – is needed to work against the mutual attraction between the particles and spread them out. The reverse process – condensation – involves the particles coming together. This process gives out energy – again, latent heat – so when a gas condenses to a liquid, energy is released. Just as with melting and freezing, the First Law of Thermodynamics (see Section 4.1.2) predicts that, at a given temperature, the energy required to change a given mass of liquid into gas is the same as the energy obtained when the same mass of gas condenses into a liquid.

You may be wondering what causes the particles in a gas to move in all directions and what affects their speed. The key factor here is the temperature. At the particle level, temperature is a measure of the average energy of the random motions of the particles: the greater the temperature, the greater the average energy of motion and the greater the random speeds of the particles. If a solid, liquid or gas is heated, at the particle level the energy of random motion increases, which we see as a rise in temperature (provided no melting or evaporation occurs instead). If we heat a solid, the constituent particles vibrate more energetically about their fixed positions. Eventually the particles vibrate so violently that they can leave their fixed positions: the solid melts to give a liquid. As this liquid is heated, the particles in it move around more quickly: the energy of their random motion has increased. At the boiling temperature these particles are moving so fast that they can easily free themselves from each other and the liquid is completely converted into a gas. Further heating of the gas causes the gaseous particles to move around even more quickly.

● What happens at the particle level when the atmosphere, the ocean and the land absorb radiation?

◉ When particles in the atmosphere absorb solar radiation their energy is increased, which leads to the gas particles moving around more quickly. Similarly, when water particles in the ocean absorb radiation they start moving around more quickly. When solid material on the Earth's surface absorbs radiation, each particle vibrates about a particular point more energetically.

At this stage, you might wonder how evaporation can occur at temperatures that are well below the boiling temperature of the liquid. This is explained by the fact that the energy of the random motion of the particles in a liquid is not the same for all the particles. Collisions between particles can lead to some of them having instantaneous energy that is very high, or very low, even though most of them have energy that is near the average. The particles with very high energy can overcome the forces of attraction between them. If they do this when they are in the surface layer, they can escape from the liquid and hence turn to gas (Figure 5.3).

5.1.2 The pressure of being a gas

Consider the particles of gas (i.e. air) in an inflatable bicycle tyre. They are moving around and colliding with the walls of the tyre. When we pump up the tyre we increase the amount of gas inside it: that is, we add more particles. As we put in more particles there are more collisions, which has the effect of pushing the walls outwards. Eventually we put in so many particles that their collisions with the tyre walls hold them firmly in place, forming a cushion of air for us to ride on.

Let's look at this effect in a little more detail. Figure 5.4 shows several particles colliding with a surface, such as a tyre wall. The particles are moving in all directions in a chaotic fashion and bouncing off the walls. Each time a particle hits the wall it exerts a force on the wall, just as when a ball bounces off a bat or racquet. There are so many particles in a tyre that there is a continuous shower of particles bombarding the walls, leading to a steady force, which holds the tyre in shape. We say the tyre is 'under pressure' or that the gas 'exerts a pressure'.

In scientific terms, the pressure on the small section of the wall shown in Figure 5.4 is defined as the force acting on this section divided by the surface area of this section of the wall:

$$\text{pressure} = \frac{\text{force on the surface}}{\text{area of that surface}} \qquad \text{[5.1]}$$

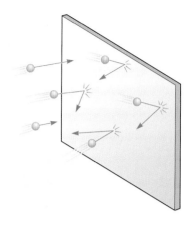

Figure 5.4 A gas exerts a force on a surface, such as the wall of a tyre, as a result of collisions.

It is important to note that the pressure is the same throughout the tyre. If it were not, the pressure imbalance would force some of the particles from the high-pressure zone to the low-pressure zone, to make the pressure uniform everywhere.

For a gas contained in a fixed volume, the higher the temperature, the higher the pressure. Why does the pressure depend on temperature? The pressure depends not only on how many particles are present in the fixed volume but also on how often and how hard the particles hit the walls. This depends on how fast they are travelling, and temperature is a measure of this. As we heat up a gas, the particles in it will, on average, move more quickly. This means the force from their impact with the walls will be greater, and the particles will also collide with the walls more often. Both these factors lead to an increase in the overall force on the walls of the container. This means the pressure increases.

Many units are used to express pressure, at least four of which are in common use. Motor vehicle drivers may be familiar with those used for measuring the air pressure in tyres. You may have seen pounds per square inch or p.s.i. (a typical car tyre pressure is about 30 p.s.i.) or perhaps the bar, where a pressure of 30 p.s.i. is equivalent to about 2 bars. Weather forecasters often quote atmospheric pressure in millibars (mb), where 1000 mb = 1 bar. Another unit commonly used to describe pressure is the pascal (Pa) or, perhaps more commonly, the hectopascal (hPa), which is 100 Pa. As 1 mb = 1 hPa, it follows that pressures are numerically the same, whether they are quoted in mb or hPa. A fourth unit of pressure sometimes used in meteorological contexts is 'millimetres of mercury', the origins of which need not be explained here.

5.2 The vertical profile of the Earth's atmosphere

Now that you are more familiar with gases, we can start to make sense of the atmosphere, which in turn will help you to understand better the ways in which it affects the GMST. The atmosphere can be divided into four layers, as shown in Figure 5.5, which are described in more detail in Section 5.2.1. The lower atmosphere is known as the troposphere; this is where we live and it is also the region where weather systems operate. Above this there is the stratosphere, where much air travel occurs, and higher still there are the mesosphere and the thermosphere.

Figure 5.5 The variation of temperature (orange line) with altitude (height above sea-level), showing the different layers in the atmosphere with approximate altitudes. The thickness of the troposphere and the actual temperature values vary with latitude, location and season. Note that neither axis is a continuous scale.

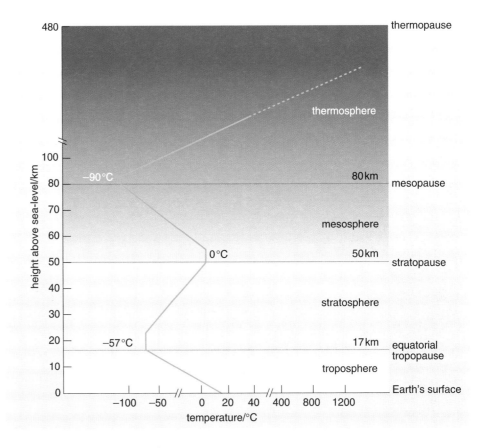

5.2.1 The four major layers

The troposphere

The troposphere is the lowest region of the atmosphere. Throughout the troposphere, the temperature decreases with altitude at a more or less steady rate of about 6 °C per kilometre, known as the environmental lapse rate. This rate varies from place to place and is particularly sensitive to topography. The temperature reaches a minimum at an altitude of between 10 and 20 km. This level is called the tropopause and it defines the boundary between the troposphere and the stratosphere. Temperatures in the tropopause can be around −57 °C. The height of the tropopause depends on the amount of solar radiation, and is lowest at the poles and highest at the Equator (Figure 5.6).

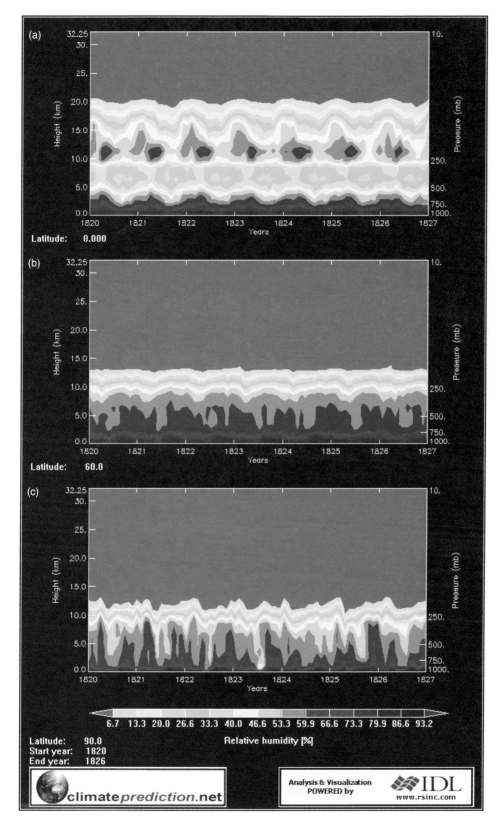

Figure 5.6 A modelled vertical section through the atmosphere showing how the relative humidity, a measure of the amount of water in the atmosphere (see Box 4.1), varies over seven years at three different latitudes: (a) the Equator; (b) 60° N; and (c) the North Pole. Because the stratosphere is dry compared with the troposphere, the transition to dark blue in the figures indicates the approximate position of the tropopause.

● What is the height of the tropopause at each of the latitudes in Figure 5.6?

◉ In these model calculations, the tropopause is at about 20 km altitude over the Equator, at 13 km at 60 °N and at about 11 km at the North Pole, based on the lowest humidity contour.

The term 'troposphere' comes from the Greek 'tropos', which means to turn or churn, because in the troposphere there is the greatest amount of atmospheric churning or mixing as a result of convection. Almost all the weather phenomena, including cloud formation and precipitation (which are discussed in Section 5.3) occur in the troposphere. This is also the part of the atmosphere that contains the most water vapour. About 80% of the mass of the atmosphere is in the troposphere.

The stratosphere

As its name suggests, the stratosphere is stratified or layered in a stable manner, in contrast to the mixing that goes on in the troposphere.

● From Figure 5.5, how does temperature vary within the stratosphere?

◉ The temperature increases from around −57 °C at the base of the stratosphere to about 0 °C at the stratopause, the top of the stratosphere.

Overall this is a more stable temperature situation than in the troposphere and there is virtually no convection. However, exceptionally vigorous convection in the troposphere can cause storm clouds to 'punch through' the tropopause into the stratosphere (Figure 5.7). Unlike the relatively wet troposphere, the stratosphere is dry (Figure 5.6), so any overshooting cloud soon evaporates. The temperature of 0 °C at the stratopause (Figure 5.5) is an annual average for middle latitudes. The warming in the higher layers of the stratosphere is caused by the absorption of ultraviolet (UV) radiation by the ozone layer. Most of the ozone is concentrated between 20 and 30 km altitude and absorbs about 90% of potentially harmful UV radiation, except in the polar regions, where it has been thinned by human-produced chemicals (Figure 5.8). Although the production of ozone-destroying gases has been curtailed under international agreements, concentrations of the gases in the stratosphere are only now reaching their peak. It will be many decades before the ozone hole is no longer a problem.

Figure 5.7 Sharp boundaries between air masses, such as this one photographed by astronauts on board the Space Shuttle, are often the focus of development for severe thunderstorms. The 'anvil tops' of these thunderstorms are estimated to be in the stratosphere at an altitude exceeding 18 km (see Figure 5.5). The distribution and impact of such high clouds is a significant challenge to modelling the Earth's energy budget and climate.

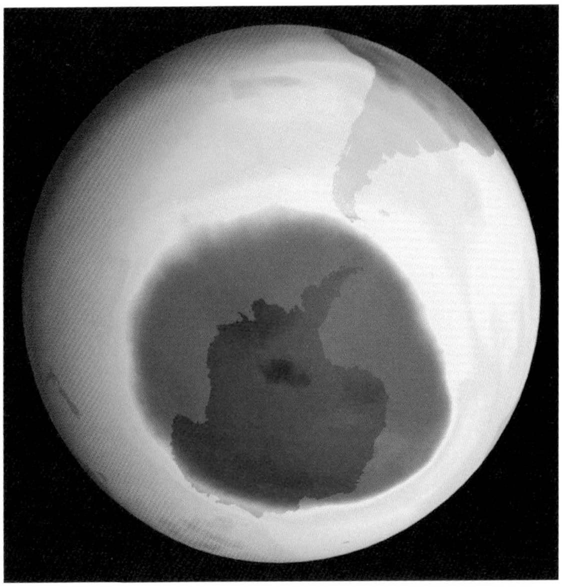

Figure 5.8 The ozone 'hole' over the Antarctic on 3 September 2000. Blue indicates low ozone levels and red indicates high ozone levels.

The mesosphere

The mesosphere, or middle region of the atmosphere, extends to the mesopause at about 80 km altitude. Here temperatures can be around –90 °C. As with the troposphere, the cooling with increasing altitude (Figure 5.5) can give rise to convection and very thin clouds called noctilucent clouds can form, particularly over the polar regions in the summer (see Figure 5.9).

The thermosphere

As its name suggests, the thermosphere has the highest temperatures (Figure 5.5), although the concept is a little misleading because the atmosphere here is so thin, i.e. contains very few particles. The direct effect of high-energy radiation from the Sun makes the particles extremely energetic, just as they would be if they were heated to very high temperatures. Charged particles from the Sun interacting with particles in the thermosphere cause them to glow, creating the Aurora Borealis near the North Pole and the Aurora Australis near the South Pole. (The auroras occur near the poles because that is where the Earth's magnetic field concentrates the charged particles from the Sun.)

It is difficult to define where the top of the atmosphere is because it gradually thins to the almost pure vacuum of space. This is beautifully illustrated in another photograph from the Space Shuttle (Figure 5.9), showing the cloud layers of the troposphere overlain by a stratified stratosphere, passing imperceptibly up through the mesosphere and thermosphere to the blackness of space and the crescent Moon in the distance.

Figure 5.9 The edge of the Earth. This image shows the transition from the rim of the Earth at the bottom into the orange-coloured troposphere, the lowest and densest portion of the Earth's atmosphere. The troposphere ends abruptly at the tropopause, which appears as the sharp boundary between the orange-coloured troposphere and blue-coloured stratosphere. Silvery-blue noctilucent clouds are far above this boundary in the mesosphere. The thin thermosphere is too tenuous to be noticeable.

5.2.2 The density and pressure profiles

In Section 5.1 we said that a gas will expand to fill its container: that is, the particles will spread throughout the available volume. So why doesn't the atmosphere spread out into space and disappear from the Earth's surface?

The answer is gravity. Just as an apple will fall to the ground under the influence of gravity, so the gas particles in the atmosphere are attracted to the Earth. If the particles were stationary they would fall straight down to the Earth's surface to form a thin dense layer. However, because they are jostling around there is a 'layer' of gas particles around the Earth. The number of particles in a given volume (such as a cubic metre) is greatest at the surface of the Earth and decreases as we move away from the surface. This decrease is shown in Table 5.1, and schematically in Figure 5.5, where the transition in the background tint represents the decrease in particle numbers. Like any other gas, the air exerts a pressure, which depends on the number of particles in a given volume and on the temperature. The air pressure at different altitudes is also shown in Table 5.1. As you can see, the pressure is already less than one-third of the sea-level value by the height of Mount Everest and barely ten-millionths of the sea-level value at the mesopause.

Table 5.1 The number of particles in a cubic metre of air, and the air pressure, at different altitudes.

Altitude/km	Zone	Number of particles in a cubic metre of air	Air pressure/bar
0	sea-level	2.6×10^{25}	1.0
10	top of Mount Everest, troposphere	8.7×10^{24}	2.8×10^{-1}
40	stratosphere	8.9×10^{22}	3.2×10^{-3}
80	mesopause	5.2×10^{20}	1.3×10^{-5}
120	thermosphere	1.2×10^{18}	4.6×10^{-8}
160	thermosphere	3.8×10^{16}	2.7×10^{-9}

You may recall the definition of pressure in equation 5.1 as the force on a surface divided by the area of that surface. In the case of atmospheric pressure, the relevant force is the weight of the overlying atmosphere pressing down on it because of gravity. When we measure the pressure of the atmosphere we are really measuring not only how much air there is (its mass) but also the strength of gravity at that point. (We are not usually aware of it but the strength of gravity varies slightly from place to place on the Earth's surface, depending on the type and amount of rock at each location.)

5.3 Water in the atmosphere

In Section 5.1 we introduced some of the properties of a gas, and in Section 5.2 we described how the mixture of gases that comprise the atmosphere are distributed with height. We shall discuss the composition of the atmosphere in greater detail in Chapter 7 but we have already encountered several times in this book one of the most important gases for weather and climate – water vapour.

● Can you recall an example of how water vapour effects energy transport in the atmosphere?

* The latent heat of vaporisation extracts energy from the Earth's surface as water is converted into water vapour, and releases it again at high altitude as the latent heat of condensation, when the vapour cools and condenses (Section 4.1.2).

Water is also crucial to life on Earth, determining where life can be supported, depending on whether there is too much water (flood) or too little (drought). Clearly, we need to know what influences the amount of water vapour in the atmosphere and whether this amount varies in the short and the long term. This, in turn, requires us to examine how water gets into and out of the atmosphere. As you might expect, we must first look at how water, in all its various forms, is distributed on the Earth.

● Give some examples of the different forms in which water exists around the Earth.

* Water exists in the gaseous state (water vapour) in the atmosphere; as liquid water droplets or solid ice crystals in clouds; as liquid water in the oceans, lakes, rivers and underground; and as solid ice in snow, glaciers and ice-sheets.

5.3.1 Clouds

One of the most obvious manifestations of water vapour in the atmosphere is the formation of clouds, although clouds themselves are composed of tiny liquid water droplets or ice crystals, not water vapour. In Section 4.1.2 we introduced the notion of saturation, i.e. that there is a maximum amount of water vapour that a parcel of air can contain. This maximum amount decreases as the temperature decreases, and so the amount of water in the air coming off an ocean at, say, 20 °C will probably be too much for the air to hold at, say, 10 °C. As our discussion of the vertical profile of the atmosphere showed (Section 5.2.1), the temperature decreases with height, so water vapour that rises in the atmosphere through convection does indeed cool. Once it cools sufficiently, the water vapour condenses, producing a cloud of tiny liquid water droplets, or ice crystals if the temperature is low enough (e.g. at high altitude).

When water vapour condenses, it does so preferentially around solid particles or 'nuclei' such as pollen grains, dust or salt from sea spray. Condensation can also occur on minute droplets called aerosols, many of which are sulfur compounds, notably sulfuric acid formed from water vapour and sulfur dioxide that is emitted from volcanoes or produced by industrial processes. The freezing point of water is 0 °C at sea-level but decreases if the air pressure is lowered. As the air pressure decreases with increasing height in the atmosphere (Table 5.1), the freezing temperature of water also decreases, to less than 0 °C at higher altitude. Water droplets can exist in clouds at temperatures down to –12 °C; between –12 and –30 °C, there can be a mixture of water droplets and ice crystals; at temperatures below –30 °C, ice crystals predominate; and at temperatures below –40 °C, clouds consist entirely of ice crystals. As the droplets (or, more usually, ice crystals) get larger and heavier, air currents associated with convection can no longer support them and they fall out of the cloud. On falling through lower, warmer air, the ice crystals often melt again to form liquid drops of rain.

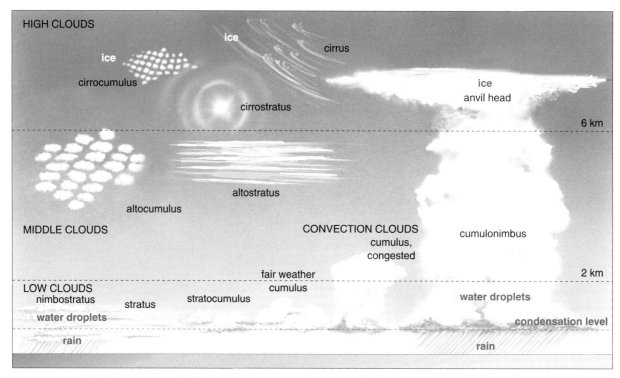

HIGH CLOUDS

ice
cirrus

ice
cirrocumulus

cirrostratus

ice
anvil head

6 km

altostratus

altocumulus

MIDDLE CLOUDS

CONVECTION CLOUDS
cumulus,
congested

cumulonimbus

2 km

fair weather
cumulus

LOW CLOUDS
nimbostratus

stratus

stratocumulus

water droplets

water droplets

condensation level

rain

rain

Figure 5.10 Various types of clouds and their characteristic levels and/or extents in the atmosphere.

Figure 5.10 shows that clouds have a variety of forms. For example, cumulus and cumulonimbus, which are associated with convection, have flat bottoms (marking the height at which condensation began) and bubbly tops, whereas stratus clouds, formed by the more gentle uplift of air at a front (weather fronts are discussed in Section 6.1) or as a result of the presence of mountains, are layered. Wispy cirrus-type clouds are made of ice and are usually associated with flow in jet streams, which are high-speed air currents that circle the globe (see Section 6.3). Cumulus-type clouds consist of water droplets, although the tops of towering cumulonimbus clouds consist of ice crystals. Stratus-type clouds – which we call fog when they occur at ground level – can be made of either ice or water droplets. Stratiform clouds tend to cover a large area, so rain from them is more persistent than that from individual clouds. Thunderstorms, although localised, tend to produce heavy rain because the convection associated with a thunderstorm is particularly vigorous.

Clouds are an important part of the climate system but, as we shall see in Chapter 8, they are relatively poorly understood, which means they are particularly difficult to represent accurately in a climate model. The formation of rain is a complex process, which is why it is so difficult to predict, particularly in models that try to forecast over months and years. This is because water vapour in the atmosphere is so crucial for atmospheric processes and any small uncertainty in modelling will be compounded as the model simulation proceeds.

5.3.2 Precipitation

One of the most important aspects of the occurrence of water on the Earth is the fact that it is not static. There is a continuous exchange of water between

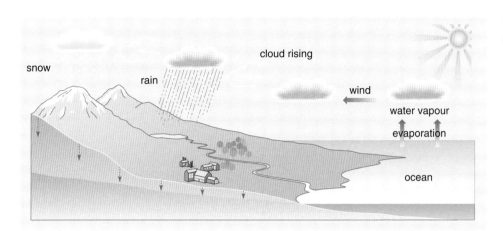

Figure 5.11 A schematic diagram of the water cycle.

the oceans, the atmosphere, lakes, streams, surface ice and clouds. This system of exchange is called the water cycle (Figure 5.11).

One of the more obvious ways in which we see water being exchanged within the water cycle is when it rains. The more general term for rain is precipitation, which includes any form of water, liquid or solid, that originates from the atmosphere and ends up on the ground. Examples include rain, hail, snow, dew and frost. If you want to know more about the different origins of hail and snow, you could read Box 5.1.

Box 5.1 Hail and snow

Hail forms when a water droplet is circulated round and round through different zones of temperature and humidity by the convection within a cumulonimbus cloud. It goes through a series of freezing, melting and further freezing, which builds up successive layers of ice on what may have been initially a small droplet. The requirement for strong convection means that hailstorms are largely restricted to middle latitudes, where intense solar heating of the Earth's surface, and subsequent heating of the air, drives such strong convection (see Figure 4.3). Although convection is strong in the tropics, the high temperatures, particularly at lower altitudes, tend to melt the hailstones before they hit the ground, while near the poles there is so little heating of the ground by solar radiation that strong convection cells are unlikely to be formed.

Snow begins to form as water vapour freezes around microscopic dust and aerosol particles. These particles act as nuclei around which crystallisation occurs. The individual ice crystals coalesce and bond together, forming snowflakes. As a snowflake grows it becomes heavier and starts to fall out of the cloud. Many snowflakes melt as they fall into warmer air but the melting process requires energy (latent heat – see Section 4.1.2) and so the melting process cools the surrounding air such that subsequent flakes have a greater probability of reaching the ground. Warm air can hold more moisture than cold air, so snow tends to form only when temperatures are just below freezing. If temperatures are much lower the air is too dry and large flakes cannot form. Also, because snow forms only close to the freezing point, small changes in temperature can make the difference between it snowing or raining, making numerical modelling of exactly when, where and how much snow will fall very difficult.

We have seen how convection causes warm, moist air to rise and cool, forming clouds (Figure 5.11), but air masses can also rise by physical deflection over mountains. In Scotland, the Lake District of northern England and in Wales there are mountains close to the west coast, and the air needs to rise to get over them. As the air rises, its temperature decreases at a rate called the adiabatic lapse rate. Whereas the environmental lapse rate (Section 5.2.1) indicates how the temperature differs at different altitudes in the atmosphere at one instant, the adiabatic lapse rate indicates how the temperature of a given air mass falls if its altitude increases (and if no energy is gained or lost). The adiabatic lapse rate for dry air is 10 °C per kilometre, whereas rising saturated air cools at an average rate of only about 6 °C per kilometre, a lower rate because of the release of latent heat.

● To pass over the Highlands of Scotland, air needs to rise by about 1000 m. By how many degrees will saturated air cool?

◍ Since the air cools at an average of 6 °C per kilometre, a rise of 1000 m corresponds to a cooling of about 6 °C.

In Chapter 6, we shall see how global wind patterns form and what their role is in transporting energy and water vapour around the Earth. However, here it is useful at least to begin to consider the role of winds in transporting water vapour, since that determines how much precipitation occurs and where it falls. Figure 5.12 shows the average wind directions for Europe during winter. (Average pressures are also shown.) If you are interested in knowing how wind is measured, see Box 5.2.

Box 5.2 Measuring wind speed and direction

Wind speed is measured with an anemometer, which usually consists of conical cups on the end of rotor arms (usually three) mounted on a vertical spindle. The conical cups 'catch' the wind and cause the rotor to move. The rotation is displayed on a dial calibrated in, for example, metres per second (m s^{-1}). Air does not flow freely across the ground because of friction. To obtain a standard wind-speed measurement that is unaffected by this, the anemometer should be mounted 10 metres above the ground surface.

Wind direction is measured with a weather vane, consisting of a horizontally mounted metal arm with a small pointer at one end and a large metal plate at the other aligned along the pointer arm. Movements of the vane are transmitted to an anemograph, which provides a continuous record of wind movement. In weather reports the average over a few minutes is given and is expressed in degrees read clockwise from true north to the nearest 10°. It is the direction *from* which the wind is blowing, not *where* it is heading, that is reported.

● Does Figure 5.12 show a dominant wind direction for the UK in winter?

◍ Figure 5.12 clearly shows that the UK is influenced by westerly winds – i.e. winds that blow from the west – which move air from over the Atlantic Ocean, across the west coast and towards the east.

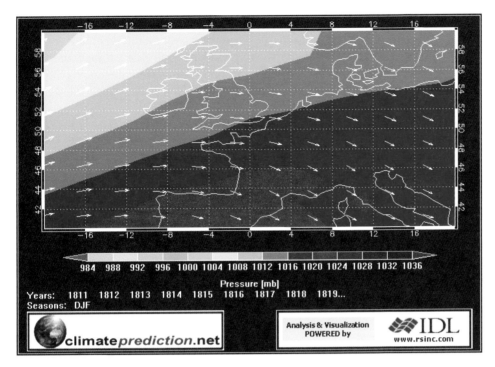

Years: 1811   1812   1813   1814   1815   1816   1817   1810   1819...
Seasons: DJF

climate*prediction*.net

Analysis & Visualization POWERED by   IDL
www.rsinc.com

Figure 5.12 Modelled map of the average seasonal pressure and wind directions for central and western Europe for December, January and February. The arrows show wind direction and the length of the arrows is proportional to the wind strength.

This air flow over Europe from the Atlantic Ocean is moist. Moisture-laden air that is forced to rise by the presence of mountains will cool and, being cooler, can no longer hold as much moisture. If cooling is sufficient, condensation will occur, clouds will form and rain or snow will fall (Figure 5.13). As a result, the elevated areas of Scotland, the Lake District in England and Wales are characterised by more cloud formation and a higher rainfall than would otherwise be the case. Cloud and rain produced when moist air is forced upwards by mountains, rather than by convection, are called orographic cloud and orographic rain. By contrast, air subsiding over a lee slope descends to lower altitudes where the pressure is higher and warms up. Having no moisture source, it may become very dry, resulting in a rain shadow. Hence, climatic conditions are affected not only by the distribution of land and sea but also by the shape of the land masses in the vertical dimension – their topography – and by their interaction with the prevailing winds.

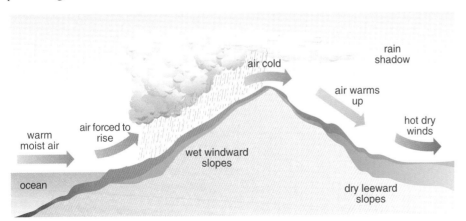

Figure 5.13 Orographic precipitation: mountains cause moisture-laden air to rise, with the result that the windward slopes are wet and well vegetated. On the leeward side, the dry air warms up as it descends to lower altitude where the air pressure is higher, creating a warm, dry area of rain shadow.

These conditions are replicated in many other locations around the world on all scales – on small volcanic islands in mid-ocean and over mountain chains. For example, in southwestern USA, the western slopes of the Coast Range and the Sierra Nevada receive ample precipitation from the moisture-laden winds blowing off the Pacific; to the southeast of these mountains, in their lee, there are the desert regions of Nevada and eastern California.

- Apart from the physical barrier of mountains, is there any other mechanism that might enhance the rise of air masses when they are forced over high ground?

- As the moisture condenses, it releases latent heat which warms the air mass and makes it rise further.

5.3.3 Amounts of precipitation

How much precipitation falls on average on the Earth's surface in a year? To answer this question we start by measuring the precipitation at many locations. To measure precipitation, all forms of water must be included – rain, snow, hail, dew and frost. The measurement of precipitation is described in Box 5.3. We pick up the discussion of variations in precipitation with time and place in Section 5.4.

Box 5.3 Measuring precipitation

A rain gauge in its most basic form is simply a straight-sided container into which rain, or any other form of precipitation, falls. The amount (depth in millimetres) that has fallen in a specified time is measured and the rain gauge is emptied before another recording interval starts. Some distance below the rim of the container there is a funnel that passes through into a collecting vessel. The narrow neck of the funnel reduces the evaporation from the collecting vessel. The rim of the gauge is well above the top of the funnel to reduce losses from splashing as rain hits the funnel's sloping sides. Similarly, the top of the gauge's rim is positioned 30.5 cm above any surface to eliminate any over-reading by rain splashing into the gauge. For the same reason the gauge should be sited well away from any buildings or other objects that may affect the trajectory of any precipitation.

While this design provides totals over a given interval of time (e.g. daily measurements), it does not provide continuous detailed measurements of individual storms. This requires a recording gauge, which commonly consists of two small buckets on a kind of see-saw mechanism such that when one bucket is filled to a specified amount it tips and the other bucket swings into the position for collecting further precipitation. The filling of each bucket alternates and each tip of the bucket is registered either electronically to a central data-collecting point or on a paper chart.

A modern supplement to rain gauges is the use of radar to plot the amount (intensity) and location of individual precipitation events.

We know from personal experience that the precipitation in one week is usually somewhat different from the precipitation in another week. Even the precipitation in one year is usually different from that in the preceding or following year. Therefore, to reduce the effect of year-to-year variations, the annual precipitation is averaged over a sequence of years. This average is called the mean annual precipitation. In Chapter 2 you saw something similar is done to obtain the mean surface temperature. Figure 5.14 shows how the mean annual precipitation varies across the British Isles.

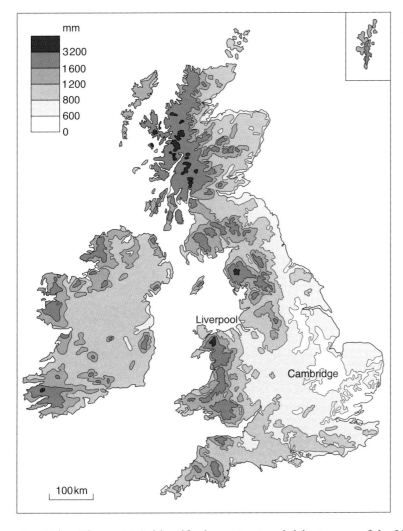

Figure 5.14 Mean annual precipitation across the British Isles. Different shades are used to represent different ranges of mean annual precipitation.

● Using Figure 5.14, identify the wettest and driest areas of the UK.

◔ The wettest parts are those coloured darkest blue, which correspond to the western coastal mountains of Scotland, the Lake District and Wales.
The driest areas are those coloured white, particularly around East Anglia.

● How do you think the data in Figure 5.14 were obtained?

◔ The precipitation at many sites was measured over several years, and the mean annual precipitation was calculated for each site as an average precipitation per year. If the mean annual precipitation is measured in sufficient places, a picture can be built up of how the precipitation varies across the British Isles.

Although precipitation varies on a day-to-day basis, when it is totalled over a whole year the short-term fluctuations are smoothed out so that the annual precipitation, although varying somewhat, should be more consistent from year to year. However, although totalling over a year provides data that are less prone to erratic variation, it obscures patterns within the year.

Figure 5.15 shows how the mean monthly precipitation varies during the year for Liverpool and Cambridge in England and New Delhi in India; Figure 1.2b gave similar data for London. The horizontal axis shows the months of the year, from January to December. The width of each column denotes a whole month, and each column is the same width. The vertical axis indicates the amount of precipitation for each month, measured in millimetres, based on the readings for several years. For example, if the mean for a particular month was based on the readings for five years, this would be the total precipitation during that month over the five years, divided by five.

● How does the precipitation vary over the year in Liverpool, Cambridge and New Delhi?

◉ Figure 5.15 shows that the precipitation at the two UK sites is reasonably uniform over the year, February to June being slightly drier than the rest of the year. In contrast, New Delhi has very high rainfall from June to September and little for the rest of the year.

So far, we have looked at precipitation at specific locations. Figure 5.14 shows how the precipitation varies across the British Isles but, to get a world picture, we need to use mean values from around the globe: these are shown in Figure 1.3.

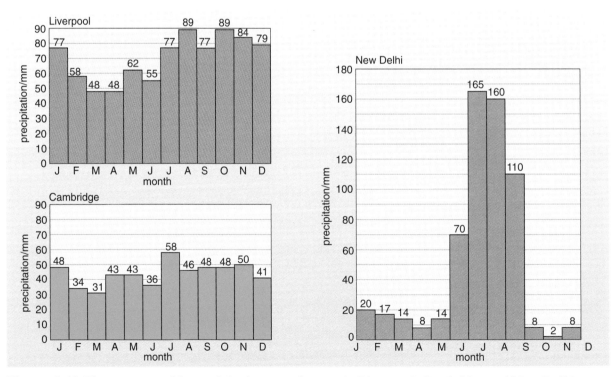

Figure 5.15 The mean monthly precipitation over the year in Liverpool, Cambridge and New Delhi.

- How might we calculate a value for the global mean annual precipitation?

- In a similar way to determining the global mean surface temperature, we can measure the global mean annual precipitation by:

  - choosing a range of representative sites, including over the oceans
  - measuring the annual precipitation (in millimetres) at each site for several years to give the mean annual precipitation for each site
  - taking the average of the mean annual precipitation for each site to get the global mean annual precipitation.

The resulting value of the global mean annual precipitation is equivalent to a depth of about 1000 mm of liquid water per year over the whole surface of the Earth.

There is a different way of expressing the global mean annual precipitation.

- The total volume of a depth of 1000 mm of liquid water at the Earth's surface is the area of the Earth's surface multiplied by this depth. Given that the area of the Earth's surface is 5.1×10^{14} m^2, calculate the total volume of liquid water.

- Because 1000 mm = 1 m, the total volume is $1 \text{ m} \times (5.1 \times 10^{14} \text{ m}^2)$, which is 5.1×10^{14} m^3.

The density of liquid water at the Earth's surface is 1000 kg m^{-3}. This number is the mass in kilograms of one cubic metre. Therefore, the total mass of the liquid water is the density multiplied by the total volume:

$$\text{total mass} = (1000 \text{ kg m}^{-3}) \times (5.1 \times 10^{14} \text{ m}^3)$$

$$= (10^3 \times 5.1 \times 10^{14}) \times (\text{kg m}^{-3} \times \text{m}^3) = 5.1 \times 10^{17} \text{ kg}$$

The global mean annual precipitation of 1000 mm is thus equivalent to 5.1×10^{17} kg of water. This way of expressing the amount is very suitable for our discussion, with its emphasis on water in all its various forms. We can specify a mass of water regardless of whether it is vapour, liquid or one of the various solid forms, from fluffy snow to ice. Thus, if 1 kg of water vapour condenses, we get 1 kg of liquid water, and so on.

- From Figure 5.15, calculate the mean annual precipitation in Liverpool, Cambridge and New Delhi.

- The mean annual precipitation for each site is obtained by adding together the data for each month: for Liverpool it is 843 mm; for Cambridge it is 526 mm; and for New Delhi it is 596 mm.

- How do these values compare with the global mean annual precipitation of 1000 mm?

- Liverpool has a mean annual precipitation approaching the global mean. Cambridge and New Delhi are considerably drier but New Delhi is slightly wetter than Cambridge – on average!

The shortcoming of mean annual precipitation values is that they do not reveal the seasonal variations. This is particularly apparent for New Delhi, where most of the precipitation occurs in just four months.

5.4 The water cycle: what comes down must go up

We have described how precipitation originates from water in the atmosphere, but how much water is there in the whole atmosphere? If all the water in the atmosphere fell evenly as rain around the globe, the rainfall would be about 30 mm deep all over the Earth. However, we have already seen that the global mean annual precipitation is about 1 000 mm, about 30 times greater than the amount of water in the atmosphere, so why does the rain keep coming? Why doesn't the atmosphere run out of water?

5.4.1 Why the rain doesn't stop

The reason why the atmosphere doesn't run out of water is that it is constantly being replenished by evaporation and sublimation – and from now on we shall take evaporation to include sublimation. Evaporation happens around the whole globe, especially over the oceans, so it is not surprising that the water content of the atmosphere is constantly replenished.

Look at Figure 5.16, which starts to represent the water cycle as a flow diagram. We have divided the global total of water between two boxes – that in the atmosphere and that on the land or in the ocean. The masses in the boxes refer to the present estimate of water in each of them. The atmosphere and the land and ocean can be regarded as reservoirs. Here we use the term 'reservoir' as a means of collecting under one heading all water in a particular type of location. Thus the reservoir labelled 'land and ocean' refers to all water on Earth that occurs on the land and in the ocean. The numbers on the arrows connecting the reservoirs refer to the rate of movement of water from one reservoir to another, in kilograms per year (kg y^{-1}).

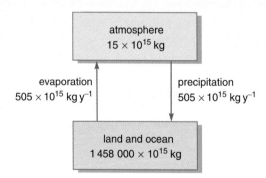

Figure 5.16 A flow diagram to show the balance between water entering the atmosphere by evaporation and water leaving the atmosphere by precipitation. The numbers in the boxes refer to the amount of water in kilograms in that particular reservoir. The numbers on the arrows refer to the rate of movement of water from one reservoir to another in kilograms per year. Note: to make comparison easier, all the numbers are written with the same power of ten: 10^{15}.

● What do you notice from Figure 5.16 about the rates of precipitation and evaporation?

⟁ The rate at which water leaves the atmosphere in the form of precipitation is the same as the rate at which water enters the atmosphere by evaporation.

This balance of water entering and leaving the atmosphere ensures that the amount of water in the atmosphere remains relatively constant, although you must remember that the system is a dynamic one with water continuously entering and leaving the atmosphere. This is another example of a steady state, in this case a *dynamic* steady state since water is still moving around the cycle, to contrast it with a *static* steady state in which all flows have stopped.

We can calculate a residence time for water in the atmosphere or any reservoir. This is the average length of time that a water molecule stays in the reservoir. The residence time depends on how big the reservoir is and the rate at which water moves into and out of it. If the reservoir is large with only a small flow of water in and out, the average length of time a water molecule stays in the reservoir is quite long. However, if there is a large flow of water in and out with only a small amount of water in the reservoir, the residence time is quite short. Figure 5.16 shows that the latter is the case for the atmosphere, for which the residence time is about 11 days. This is calculated from the mass of water in the reservoir divided by the rate at which it flows through, i.e.

$$\frac{15 \times 10^{15} \text{ kg}}{505 \times 10^{15} \text{ kg y}^{-1}} = 0.03 \text{ years or 11 days.}$$

However, you must remember that this is an *average* value: some water molecules will stay in the atmosphere for longer than 11 days and others for a shorter time.

We have already seen that energy from the Sun drives the water cycle. The Sun heats the surface of the Earth, causing water to evaporate. Subsequent cooling of the water vapour leads to condensation and precipitation. Without the Sun there would be no evaporation and thus no water cycle; the flow of water around the water cycle depends on a continuous energy input from the Sun.

5.4.2 Flows between land, ocean and atmosphere

Water is transferred from the land and oceans to the atmosphere by evaporation.

● Figure 5.17 shows the monthly evaporation of water from a lake in East Anglia in England over a year. How does the evaporation change during the year, and why do you think it varies in this way?

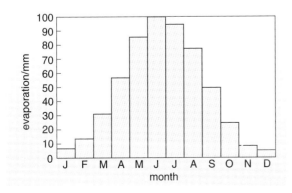

Figure 5.17 Typical monthly evaporation from a lake in East Anglia, England.

◉ The monthly evaporation is greater in the summer than in the winter. The key factor that causes this is the temperature: you will know from experience that puddles evaporate more quickly during the summer than in the winter, so the monthly total is greater in the summer.

● How does the variation in the evaporation of water from the lake in Figure 5.17 compare with the variation of the precipitation in Cambridge (a city in East Anglia) through the year, shown in Figure 5.15?

◉ There is a much greater variation in the month-by-month evaporation of water during a year than in the month-by-month precipitation. The precipitation is fairly constant throughout the year, but the evaporation peaks in the summer because of the higher temperature.

● Why are lakes in East Anglia (and elsewhere) more prone to drying up in the summer than in the winter?

◉ During the winter months precipitation is greater than evaporation and so the lakes fill up. However, during the summer months evaporation is greater than precipitation and so the lakes are more prone to drying up.

Just how easily water evaporates into the air depends on the humidity, i.e. how far the air is from being completely saturated. This is why wind and convection are other important factors controlling evaporation (Section 4.1.2), since the air in contact with liquid (or solid) water will become saturated and evaporation will slow down unless wind and convection carry away the saturated air, replacing it with less saturated air that can take up more water by evaporation.

● Is the percentage of water vapour in the air likely to be greater over the oceans or over the land, assuming the temperature is the same in both cases and that the air is not saturated?

◉ The extent of evaporation depends on the surface area of water that is in contact with the air. Clearly, this is usually greater over the oceans, so the percentage of water vapour in the atmosphere over the oceans is generally greater than that over the land.

We can demonstrate this difference by separating the parts of the water cycle that involve the land and the atmosphere over the land from those involving the oceans and the atmosphere over the oceans. This splits Figure 5.16 into the two parts shown in Figure 5.18. Note that the sum of the two atmospheric water masses, $(4 \times 10^{15}$ kg$) + (11 \times 10^{15}$ kg$)$, still equals that in Figure 5.16, i.e. 15×10^{15} kg. Similarly, the sum of the two surface water masses still equals that in Figure 5.16, as do the sums of the flow rates on the upward arrows and on the downward (precipitation) arrows (the term 'transpiration' is explained shortly). In Figure 5.18, horizontal arrows have been added to show how much water flows from the land sub-system to the atmosphere and ocean sub-system through rivers and underground water, and back again carried by winds: 36×10^{15} kg y^{-1}, the same in each case as is necessary in a dynamic steady state.

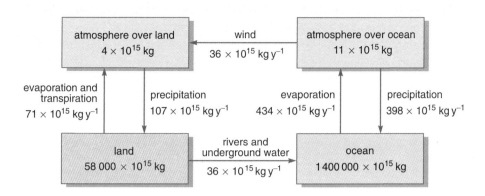

Figure 5.18 A flow diagram to show the exchange of water between the atmosphere, land and ocean in the water cycle. The numbers in the boxes refer to the mass of water in that particular reservoir. The numbers on the arrows refer to the amount of movement of water from one reservoir to another.

● Does more water evaporate from the oceans or from the land?

◉ Much more water evaporates from the oceans – about six times as much.

● There is about 2.5 times more ocean surface than land surface on the Earth. What can you infer about how readily evaporation occurs from equivalent areas of land and ocean?

◉ If evaporation from equivalent areas of the oceans and the land were the same, we would expect the total evaporation from the oceans to be about 2.5 times more than the total evaporation from the land. The fact that the total evaporation from the oceans is six times greater than the total evaporation from the land indicates that evaporation from equivalent areas occurs more than twice as readily from the oceans as from the land.

However, this is a global picture – the ratios can be very different at the regional level.

In Figure 5.18 note that, although the movement of water from the oceans to the atmosphere is labelled 'evaporation', the movement of water from the land to the atmosphere is labelled 'evaporation and transpiration'. If there were no vegetation on the land there would only be evaporation from the surfaces of open water on land – notably from rivers and lakes – and from the surface soil. The extent of evaporation from soil depends on its type and how wet it is. However, vegetation increases the amount of water transferred to the air by a process called transpiration.

Plants draw water from the soil below the surface through their roots. This water is then carried up through the stems to the leaves and lost to the air by evaporation through the many tiny pores called stomata on the surface of the leaves, through which the plant also exchanges carbon dioxide and oxygen with the atmosphere. This process is called transpiration. One result of transpiration is that nutrients are transported with the water from the roots to the stems and leaves. Another result is that significant amounts of water are moved from the soil to the air. A large oak tree, for example, transpires on average about 400 litres of water a day when in full leaf!

● Remembering that about 2.5 times as much of the Earth's surface is covered by ocean as by land, what does Figure 5.18 tell us about the relative amounts of the mean annual precipitation over the oceans and over the land?

⊛ If the mean annual precipitation over equivalent areas of ocean and land were the same, we would expect the precipitation in kilograms per year over the oceans to be about 2.5 times as large as the precipitation over the land. In fact, the total precipitation over the ocean (398) is roughly four times greater than the total precipitation over the land (107). This indicates that the mean annual precipitation over the ocean is greater than the mean annual precipitation over the land.

The cycle shown in Figure 5.18 is a closed loop in which water moves around the system, but the rate at which water enters a reservoir (such as the ocean or the atmosphere) equals the rate at which it leaves it. Therefore, overall there is no change in the total amount of water in any of the reservoirs. The water cycle is thus in a dynamic steady state: the amount of material in each reservoir is constant even though there is continuous movement of material into and out of each reservoir.

Figure 5.18 describes the location and movement of water in terms of four reservoirs – the atmosphere over the land, the atmosphere over the ocean, the ocean and the land. We can divide some of the reservoirs even further. Think for a moment about the different sorts of places where water occurs on the land. Obvious land reservoirs are rivers and lakes, and we mentioned the presence of water in the soil earlier. There are also huge amounts of water in ice-sheets, glaciers and snow. Figure 5.19 shows a more subdivided water cycle, together with estimates of the amounts of water in each of these reservoirs and the rates of transfer. You can check that these values add up to those in Figure 5.18.

Figure 5.19 The complete water cycle. The blue dashed line indicates the water table, below which the rocks are saturated with water.

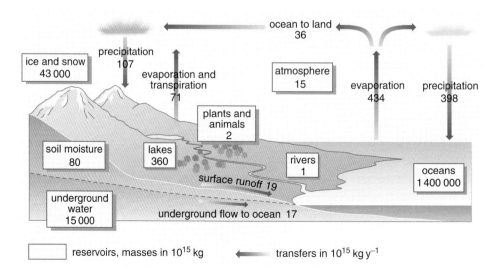

In terms of size, the largest reservoir by far is the ocean (96%), and the amount of water in the atmosphere is relatively very small. On the land the largest reservoir is ice and snow, with surface water – lakes and rivers – being quite small. What might surprise you is the amount of underground water, which is stored in pores and cracks within the rocks themselves. Water works its way down through rocks until it reaches the water table, which is the highest point below the surface where the rocks are saturated with water (Figures 5.11 and 5.19). Its depth below the ground can range from a few centimetres to hundreds of metres. Water flows from these underground sources directly into the ocean.

Residence times of water in different reservoirs are shown in Table 5.2. Although the residence time in the atmosphere is quite short, residence times in the ocean, ice-sheets and underground water are very long.

Table 5.2   Residence times of water in different reservoirs.

Reservoir	Percentage of total water	Residence time
ocean	96	about 3000 years
ice and snow	2.9	about 10 000 years
underground water	1.0	a few weeks to 10 000 years
lakes	0.025	about 10 years
soil moisture	0.005	a few weeks to 1 year
atmosphere	0.001	about 11 days
rivers	0.00007	a few weeks
plants and animals	0.00014	a few days to several months

● Why is the residence time of water in the ice and snow longer than that in the ocean, even though the ocean is a larger reservoir?

⬚ The residence time of water in ice and snow is so much longer than that in the oceans, even though the reservoir is much smaller, because the rate at which water moves from the ice into other reservoirs is so low. Once the water is frozen it will not readily flow or evaporate.

Provided that the GMST, and hence the average temperature of the atmosphere, remains fairly constant, we might expect that the amount of water in the atmosphere will also be fairly constant.

● Which processes determine how much water enters and leaves the atmosphere?

⬚ Water enters the atmosphere through evaporation and transpiration and leaves the atmosphere by precipitation.

5.4.3 The importance of water in the atmosphere

We saw in Section 4.2.1 that water plays an important role in energy transport because of the latent heat that the evaporation of water extracts from the Earth's surface and releases when water vapour condenses again in the atmosphere. Water can also condense in the atmosphere to form clouds (Section 5.3.1), which absorb and reflect radiation. Likewise, ice is highly reflective and therefore has a significant effect on albedo (Table 3.1). As you will see in Chapter 7, water vapour is also important because it is a greenhouse gas, i.e. it governs the absorption in the atmosphere of longwave infrared radiation emitted by the Earth's surface (Section 4.3.3). Although there is only a relatively small amount of water vapour in the atmosphere, it has an important effect on the surface temperature of the Earth.

There is much variability in the processes by which water vapour moves into and out of the atmosphere. We have seen how the rates of evaporation, transpiration and precipitation vary with place and with time. For example, the rate of evaporation is greater from the oceans than from the land. Similarly, you might expect evaporation and transpiration to be higher from a rainforest than from a desert. Also, Figures 5.15 and 5.17 show that, in any one place, the rates of precipitation and evaporation can vary from one month to the next. This means that, in the short term, the amount of water in the atmosphere varies greatly with time and place. However, in the medium term, the water cycle is close to a steady state, and so the mean amount of water in the atmosphere is fairly constant from one year to the next, and there is no significant trend of increasing or decreasing water vapour content in the atmosphere. Nevertheless, although the cycle may be in a steady state in the medium term, it is possible to identify ways in which the mass of water in each of the reservoirs may be altered in the long term. Just as with the GMST, the stability of the water cycle depends on the time-scale over which it is examined. One of the aims of climate modelling is to try to understand and forecast the long-term changes.

● Look again at Figure 5.19. What would be the effect of an increase in the GMST on the amount of water moving around the cycle?

◦ The cycle is driven by evaporation. If the GMST were to increase, more water would evaporate into the atmosphere, leading to more movement of water all around the cycle. If the atmosphere were also warmer, it could hold more water.

● What effect would an increased amount of water vapour in the atmosphere have on the GMST?

◦ An increase in the amount of water vapour, which is a greenhouse gas, would lead to a rise in the GMST.

Thus, an increase in the GMST would lead to an increase in the amount of water vapour in the atmosphere, which in turn would lead to a further increase in the GMST, which in turn would lead to an increase in the amount of water vapour in the atmosphere, which in turn … Thus we have two related factors that promote each other in turn, seemingly ever-increasingly (Figure 5.20). This type of behaviour, where a change in one quantity causes changes to others that eventually lead to a further change in the original quantity, is known as feedback. In this case, because the changes occur in the same direction, it is called positive feedback: that is, an increase in the original quantity leads to the quantity being increased even further. (Similarly, a decrease in some quantity that leads to a further decrease is also positive feedback.) In the case of water vapour in the atmosphere, positive feedback seems to lead to an ever-increasing rise in surface temperature – or does it?

There is another type of feedback, called negative feedback, in which an increase (or a decrease) in one quantity leads to changes in others that eventually lead to a decrease (or an increase) in the original quantity. With positive feedback, an imbalance drives the system further out of balance, whereas negative feedback returns the system to a state of balance. The water vapour content of the atmosphere is subject to several negative and positive feedback effects, some of which are poorly understood. Certainly, the single positive feedback in Figure 5.20 is far from being the complete story. For example, increased water vapour content could lead to an increase in cloud, and therefore albedo, which tends to lower the GMST. There are also the energy exchanges in evaporation and precipitation. The overall message here, though, is that it is not easy to estimate the long-term stability of the water vapour content of the atmosphere, which hampers our attempts to predict changes in the GMST.

Having looked at the structure of the atmosphere and the role of water in this chapter, we go on to look at wind and circulation patterns in Chapter 6 and the chemical composition of atmospheric gases in Chapter 7, before seeing how these factors affect weather and climate models in Chapter 8.

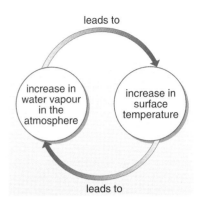

Figure 5.20 Positive feedback between the GMST and the amount of water in the atmosphere.

5.5 Summary of Chapter 5

1   The particles in a gas are relatively far apart, so there is little attraction between them. They move around rapidly in a random, chaotic manner, frequently bouncing off each other and exerting a pressure, which is defined as the force exerted on a unit area.

2   The four layers of the Earth's atmosphere are called the troposphere, stratosphere, mesosphere and thermosphere. Each layer has distinct properties. All of the weather that we experience is confined to the troposphere. In the troposphere, the temperature falls by about 6 °C per kilometre of altitude.

3   When moist air cools, the amount of water vapour it can hold falls, and tiny water droplets or ice crystals may condense out to form clouds. Condensation occurs preferentially around particles or aerosols, and if the droplets or crystals grow large enough they may fall out of the sky as precipitation. Orographic precipitation occurs when condensation is triggered by the forced cooling of water vapour as it flows up and over a mountain.

4   Water is stored in various reservoirs in the climate system, and water is continuously moving from one reservoir to another. The amount of time a molecule of water stays in a particular reservoir is called the residence time.

5   In the medium term, the water cycle is effectively in a steady state but, in the long term, the distribution of water among the reservoirs may change. If the amount of water in the atmosphere changes, this alters the contribution that water vapour makes to the greenhouse effect, which can change the GMST.

6   The water vapour content in the atmosphere is subject to several negative and positive feedback effects. Our poor understanding of many of these effects hampers our attempts to understand changes in the GMST.

6 The atmosphere in motion: winds and global circulation

'I prefer complexity to certainty, cheerful mysteries to sullen facts.'
Claude Bissell

So far in this book we have presented a fairly localised view of the atmosphere. In Chapter 5 we saw how the temperature and density vary with vertical height. We also know that water in its various forms moves from the Earth's surface to the atmosphere as a result of solar radiation-driven heating, evaporation and convection, and back again as a result of cooling, condensation and precipitation. This is an important means of transporting energy into the atmosphere from the surface. However, we have only briefly mentioned the transport of energy around the globe, which is effected by the wind. In Figure 4.10 we saw that solar radiation heats the Earth most effectively around the tropics, while the losses of longwave infrared radiation into space are fairly similar at low and high latitudes. Consequently, if we are to establish a dynamic steady state, which avoids the tropics getting hotter and the polar regions getting colder, we have to understand how energy is conveyed from low to high latitudes. In this case, the energy is carried along by large-scale movements of air, i.e. the wind. This chapter explores this process, which is called advection.

● Advection is one way of moving energy from a part of the atmosphere to another part. What are the other main ways in which energy is transported in the atmosphere?

○ Convection transports energy from the lower to the upper levels of the atmosphere. Radiation from the Earth's surface is an important means of heating the atmosphere, and vice versa. Conduction plays only a minor role, heating the lowest layers of the atmosphere where they are in contact with the Earth's surface (solid ground or bodies of water).

6.1 Surface atmospheric pressure and wind

We have talked about pressure at a microscopic level, by referring to the behaviour of the particles that make up a gas (Section 5.1). It is now time to take a macroscopic view. We want to know how large masses of air respond to pressure differences brought about by the uneven heating and cooling of different parts of the atmosphere, and the extent to which the Earth's rotation modifies this behaviour.

The pressure at the Earth's surface – often referred to as the atmospheric pressure – is not constant. It varies slightly from place to place and from day to day because of uneven heating of the Earth's surface (especially due to the different heat capacities of land and water; see Section 3.2.2) and the movement of warm air (less dense) and cold air (more dense) across the Earth's surface. Atmospheric pressure is measured using a barometer (see Box 6.1). To compare pressure readings from different places, barometers have to be adjusted to a common reference point or datum because, as we saw in Table 5.1, air pressure varies with height: about 1 millibar over a 10 metre change in height near sea-level. Variations in atmospheric pressure caused by changing weather systems (highs and lows, which are discussed below) are much more subtle and

Box 6.1 Barometers

The earliest form of barometer, which is still in use today, consists of a vertical column of mercury inside a glass tube, the top end of which is closed. The mercury column extends part-way up the tube, but there is no air between the top of the mercury column and the closed end of the tube. A space such as this, essentially devoid of gas, is called a vacuum. The open bottom end of the glass tube is submerged in an open vessel of mercury. As the atmospheric pressure varies, the force it exerts down on the surface of the mercury in the open reservoir also varies and so supports different heights of the mercury column in the glass tube.

● Apart from having to correct for the strength of local gravity, what other correction is needed to use this type of barometer in a standardised way, so that readings can be compared from place to place and over time?

● Mercury expands as it gets warmer, and contracts as it gets cooler (the phenomenon exploited in a thermometer), so corrections have to be made for temperature.

A more modern form of barometer is the aneroid barometer, literally meaning 'without air', which consists of a collapsible metal container attached to a needle that rotates around a dial as varying air pressure causes the container to squash or expand. A barograph is a modified form of aneroid barometer in which the needle is replaced by a pen. The pen continuously records changing air pressure on a paper strip mounted on a rotating drum.

in the order of only 10 mb for every 100 km distance over the land surface. Normally, then, a pressure measurement must be corrected for its height above mean sea-level. Figure 6.1 is part of a weather report that shows how the pressure at sea-level varies across the North Atlantic and Europe. The solid curves (contours) connecting places with the same atmospheric pressure are called isobars. If corrections for the different heights were not applied, such a map would mostly reflect land heights (topography) rather than the state of the atmosphere.

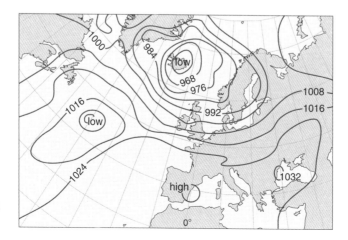

Figure 6.1 A typical map that forms part of a weather report and forecast. The numbers show the pressure at sea-level in millibars (mb) and the isobars are drawn at intervals of 8 mb.

● The weather chart in Figure 6.1 shows two 'centres' of very low atmospheric pressure (marked 'low') and sometimes called a depression. Roughly what is the pressure in these lows?

◍ The pressure will be less than that of the bounding isobar. The low on the left (over the Atlantic Ocean) has a pressure of less than 1000 mb, while in the low on the right (over Iceland) the pressure is less than 960 mb.

The variation in atmospheric pressure helps forecasters to predict the weather. 'Low pressure' is associated with unsettled weather whereas 'high pressure' is always associated with settled weather but only in the summer is that *warm* settled weather. In the eye of a hurricane, which is an extreme low-pressure area, the pressure might fall as low as 910 mb. A typical region of high pressure or 'high' in the summer has a pressure of about 1 040 mb. Changes in these patterns can have important consequences for the climate, and can also be an indicator of a changing climate.

One consequence of variations in atmospheric pressure over the Earth's surface is wind, which is caused by air attempting to flow from a region of high pressure to a region of low pressure. Winds rarely blow in a straight line but follow a path that is curved as a result of the Earth's rotation, as we shall see in Section 6.3. The exception occurs when the air flow is channelled by topography, for example down a linear valley.

Winds move air masses and air masses have different temperatures. When a mass of warm air moves into an area of cold air, it is forced to rise up over the denser cold air. The leading edge of the warm air mass is called a warm front (Figure 6.2a). Warm fronts are associated with clouds that form when moisture in the gently rising warm air condenses as the air mass cools. The first clouds to form are often cirrus clouds (see Section 5.3), then middle layer and eventually stratus clouds form, which may produce rain (see Figure 5.10).

Cold fronts form when a cold air mass moves into an area of warm air, generally in association with low-pressure systems. The arrival of the cold air forces the less dense warm air rapidly upwards (Figure 6.2b). Moisture condensing gives up latent heat, so keeping the air warm. The warm air therefore continues to rise,

Figure 6.2 (a) A warm front rises gradually over the dense cold air that it meets, producing rain over a wide area. (b) A cold front drives warm air to rise rapidly and the resulting strong convection creates thunderstorms.

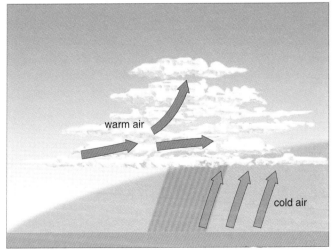

(a)

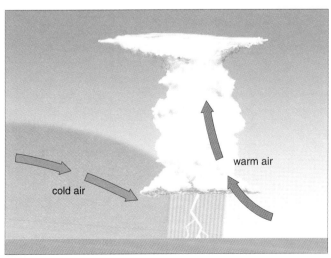

(b)

often driving powerful convection. This, in turn, creates low pressure ahead of the front and strong winds. Large cumulus and cumulonimbus clouds (see Figure 5.10) and storm systems can result. Rainfall can be intense along the cold front, with less intense rain following along behind it.

An occluded front occurs when a cold front and a warm front merge, resulting in unsettled weather.

The different rates of heating and cooling of various parts of both the Earth's surface and the atmosphere lead to pressure variations between parts of the atmosphere. As pressure is a force per unit area (Section 5.1.2), high-pressure air pushes against low-pressure air and winds result. In this section, we have seen some of the effects of this, such as winds of various strengths and the creation of fronts where one air mass pushes into another. In Section 5.3.2 we saw how orographic precipitation is caused when wind carrying moist air runs into mountains. However, out of these seemingly local effects, recognisable patterns of behaviour emerge on a global scale that systematically move energy as heat from low latitudes towards the poles. The rest of this chapter is concerned with explaining such large-scale movements of air and their importance for weather and climate modelling.

6.2 Movement by convection and advection

Convection, pressure differences and the associated winds we considered above mean that the Earth's atmosphere is not static. There is a continuous movement of air not only vertically between levels in the atmosphere but also horizontally around the Earth. The ultimate cause of this horizontal movement is the uneven heating of the Earth's atmosphere and surface.

● Why is the Earth's surface heated unevenly?

◌ In equatorial regions the Sun is high in the sky for much of each day, whereas in the polar regions it never reaches far above the horizon. Consequently, over a year, the solar radiation received per unit area of surface is greater in equatorial regions than in polar regions (see Figure 3.17), and so the polar regions are cooler.

We have seen that warm air rises or, to be more precise, air that is warmer than its surroundings, and is therefore less dense, rises. As the analogy of the pan of water demonstrates (Figure 4.1), the convective 'bulk mixing' of water distributes the heat supplied at the bottom of the pan, so that eventually all of the water becomes warm. This is the same for the atmosphere: when air is warmed by contact with a warm ocean or land surface and rises, it is replaced by cooler air which, in turn, is also warmed and rises (Figure 4.3). Unfortunately, in reality two factors complicate this simple view of convection: first, air is compressible; and, second, it contains variable amounts of water vapour, as we saw in Chapter 5. We address these factors in Sections 6.2.1 and 6.2.2.

6.2.1 Adiabatic expansion and contraction

A gas has internal energy associated with the random movements of its constituent particles, and this determines its temperature. When gas is compressed, the internal energy per unit volume of the gas is increased and it heats up. Similarly, gas cools –

i.e. decreases in energy per unit volume – when it expands. Changes in the temperature of a gas caused by expansion and compression, and not from gaining or losing heat from the surroundings, are described as adiabatic. When warmed air rises, the atmospheric pressure it is subjected to decreases (see Table 5.1) and it cools at the adiabatic lapse rate (Section 5.3.2). However, at the same time it is entering cooler surroundings (see the orange curve in Figure 5.5 and Section 5.2.1 on the environmental lapse rate).

As long as the adiabatic decrease in temperature of the rising, expanding parcel of air is less than the decrease of temperature with height in the surrounding air, the rising parcel of air will be warmer and less dense than its new surroundings. In this case it will continue to rise and so convection will continue.

● What will happen if the adiabatic cooling of the rising air mass is sufficient to reduce its temperature to below that of the surrounding air?

⦾ It will sink back down to a level where the temperature of the air mass is the same as the surrounding air temperature and convection will stop.

6.2.2 The role of latent heat

So far, we have assumed that the rising air mass is dry but the latent heat of condensation can also strongly affect convection. As discussed in Section 5.3, rising air, particularly over the ocean, may be saturated with water vapour or become saturated as a result of adiabatic cooling (cool air can contain less water vapour than warm air). Either way, the air cannot hold the excess water as vapour (gas) and the water vapour condenses as droplets of liquid. Continued rising and associated adiabatic cooling result in cloud formation – the condensation of water vapour to produce tiny water droplets or, at higher levels in the atmosphere, ice crystals. This condensation releases latent heat to the rising air, offsetting the effect of adiabatic cooling. Therefore, humid air is convected much more readily than dry air because the condensation of water vapour releases considerable additional heat (i.e. more energy), keeping the rising air warmer and therefore less dense than the surrounding air for longer than dry air.

Rising air warmed locally by conduction and/or convection is redistributed by winds. This also redistributes energy, partly by the advection (the movement in bulk) of warm air masses into cooler regions (and vice versa), and partly by the transfer of latent heat bound up in water vapour. This latent heat is released when the water vapour condenses to form cloud in a cooler environment, perhaps thousands of kilometres from the site of evaporation. Most of this moisture comes from the oceans' surface; as we saw in Section 5.4.2, at any one time a large proportion of the water in the atmosphere has only recently evaporated from the oceans since the residence time is about 11 days. As the equatorial and tropical oceans are warmer than those in polar regions, most of the evaporation occurs at low latitudes.

The subsequent poleward transport of warm humid air is the most important way in which heat from the oceans at low latitudes is transferred to the atmosphere at higher latitudes.

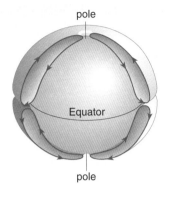

pole

Equator

pole

Figure 6.3 Simple, hypothetical atmospheric circulation system for a non-rotating, water-covered Earth.

6.3   Large-scale movements of air

So far in this chapter we have considered convection and air movements on a local scale, say a few hundred metres, or what might happen to form a cloud that covers at most a few tens of kilometres. Now we shall think about how convection affects atmospheric circulation around the whole globe. We have already seen that the Equator is the warmest part of the globe and the poles are the coolest, so we would expect that air tends to rise at the Equator and sink at the poles and that warm air rising at the Equator displaces air high in the troposphere towards the poles, where it would cool, sink and return to the Equator by surface flow. If the Earth were not rotating that is exactly what would happen (see Figure 6.3) but, in reality, this simple system is disrupted by the Earth's rotation. The rest of this section describes the consequences of the Earth's rotation for the large-scale movements of air, and how this affects the transport of water vapour and energy in the atmosphere. The Coriolis effect is central to all of these consequences (see Box 6.2).

Box 6.2   *The Coriolis effect*

The Earth rotates on its axis once every 24 hours. A person standing at the Equator travels the circumference of the Earth – 40 030 km – in just 24 hours, which works out at approximately 1668 km h^{-1}. However, the speed for a person closer to the poles is less, since a shorter distance is travelled in the same 24 hours. A person at the poles does not move at all, apart from rotating on the spot.

Now, imagine a rocket is fired from the North Pole towards the Equator. While the rocket travels in a straight line, the Earth is turning beneath it, at an increasing speed closer to the Equator. At the Equator the rocket will have its forward (southward) speed but not the eastward speed of the Earth rotating below it. From the point of view of a person on the rotating Earth, the rocket appears to drift to the west, as shown in Figure 6.4. By the time the rocket reaches the Equator, its apparent westward drift speed would be 1668 km h^{-1}. In reality, of course, it is the Earth's surface that is moving to the east, not the rocket that is moving to the west.

● Imagine now that a rocket is fired towards the North Pole from the Equator. Will it appear to move to the east or the west in relation to the Earth's surface?

● In the Northern Hemisphere it will appear to move eastward, because the rocket has the same eastward speed as the Equator, which is more than the eastward speed of the Earth below it as it travels north.

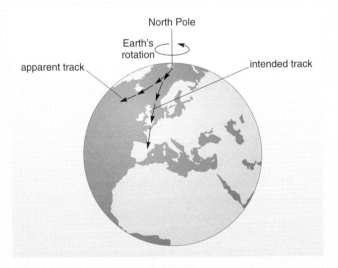

North Pole

Earth's rotation

apparent track

intended track

Figure 6.4 The Coriolis effect demonstrated by a hypothetical rocket fired south from the North Pole. It does not simply follow a line of longitude because of the Earth's rotation.

6.3.1   Global atmospheric circulation

Although the land masses and, to a lesser degree, the oceans move more or less together as the Earth turns on its axis, air masses above the Earth's surface are less well bound to it (by friction). In a sense, the Earth turns beneath the air masses.

Once set in motion, air masses would move in a straight line in the absence of other influences. However, when viewed from a rotating platform (i.e. the surface of the rotating Earth), the movements of the air masses appear curved. This deflection of the flow of winds and currents relative to the surface of the Earth is known as the Coriolis effect. This can be described as an artificial force, called the Coriolis force, pushing at right-angles to the direction of flow. In the Northern Hemisphere, the Coriolis effect deflects a flow to the right, turning it clockwise, while in the Southern Hemisphere it deflects a flow to the left, turning it anticlockwise.

The effect of deflecting winds flowing north or south from the Equator is that, by the time the winds reach about +30° or −30° of latitude, they are no longer going poleward but are flowing parallel to lines of constant latitude. As they cool, they sink at this latitude, only one-third of the way from the Equator to the poles and in contrast to the picture shown in Figure 6.3. The surface flow returns to the Equator, as shown in Figures 6.5 and 6.6, forming what are called the Trade Winds, again deflected by the Coriolis effect. This circulatory flow forms two cells of flowing air known as the Hadley cells, one each side of the Equator. The shape of the flow is helical (i.e. in the shape of a spiral), as the air also drifts westward (actually, the Earth rotates eastward beneath it) at the same time as it rises at the Equator and sinks at latitudes of 30° north and south (Figure 6.6). At the surface these winds are known as the North-East Trades and the South-East Trades.

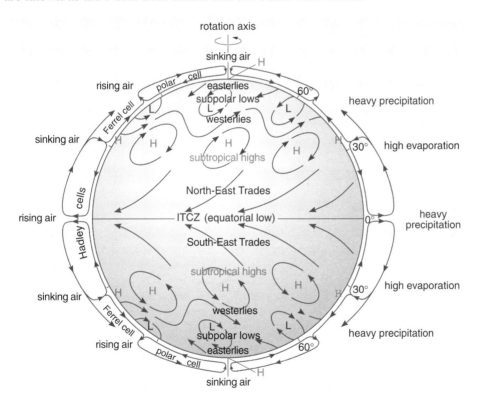

Figure 6.5 Wind system for a hypothetical water-covered, rotating Earth, showing the major surface winds and the zones of low and high pressure. In this imaginary world there are no continents to disrupt air flow, either by mountain ranges or by pressure differences caused by land heating up and cooling down quicker than water. Vertical air movements are indicated on the left-hand side and characteristic surface conditions on the right-hand side of the diagram.

Figure 6.6 The helical circulation patterns of which the Trade Winds form the surface expression; the north–south component of this helical circulation is known as the Hadley circulation; the two Hadley cells can be seen on either side of the Equator (cf. the left-hand side of Figure 6.5).

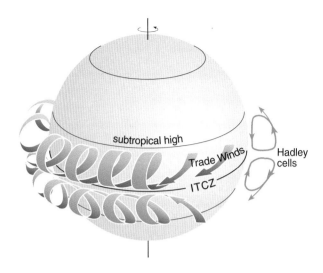

Although named after William Ferrel, the cells bearing his name are often misspelt 'Ferrell' in the literature. The Ferrel cells are not closed circulatory cells in the sense that the Hadley and polar cells are, but are a manifestation of the average behaviour of the circulation patterns at mid-latitudes.

In a similar fashion, cold air sinking at the poles is deflected on its journey towards the Equator and, by the time it reaches about 60° latitude, is flowing parallel to lines of constant latitude where it warms and returns to the pole. This circulatory flow is called the polar cell and there is one at each pole. An intermediate circulatory flow system called the Ferrel cell operates between 30° and 60° latitude and joins the other two flow systems (Figure 6.5).

The characteristic surface conditions indicated on the right-hand side of Figure 6.5 result from the fact that, while sinking air is generally dry, rising air often has a high moisture content. The most dramatic common manifestations of rising (i.e. convecting) moist air are cumulonimbus clouds, the tallest of which form near the Equator where the wind systems of the two hemispheres meet in a region called the Intertropical Convergence Zone or ITCZ (Figures 6.5 and 6.6). Here, moist air carried in the Trade Winds converges and rises, resulting in towering cloud formations (Figure 6.7) and a low surface air pressure. Cloud cover is also high around 60° latitude where air at the junction of the polar cell and the Ferrel cell is rising. In contrast, at 30° latitude where Hadley cell air is sinking and warming, through compression and greater proximity to the warmth of the Earth's surface, cloud cover is on average less and the surface pressure is high.

Figure 6.7 The Intertropical Convergence Zone (ITCZ) in the eastern Pacific is marked here by the horizontal band of cloud.

- Why do you think cloud cover tends, on average, to be higher at 60° latitude than at 30°?

- At 60° latitude air associated with the polar cell is rising. Rising air cools, moisture condenses and clouds are formed. At 30° latitude drier air is sinking.

How well do these general statements about global circulation match the real world? We pointed out that Figure 6.5 shows the *idealised* circulation pattern for a world covered in water, i.e. with no land–sea contrasts. In Figure 6.8, which shows the cloud cover for a more realistic climate model, you can see that the cloud pattern generally matches the idealised ocean world, although over Asia the ITCZ is less easily recognisable. At higher latitudes the idealised pattern is only reflected in the Southern Hemisphere where the amount of land at 60° S is minimal compared with 60° N. In the Northern Hemisphere the air flow represented in Figure 6.8 is disrupted because the land heats up and cools down more rapidly than the ocean (i.e. the land has a lower heat capacity). The faster heating of the land stimulates convection, which reduces the air pressure at the surface, producing low pressure cells more readily than over the ocean (see below). Inevitably this disturbs the idealised pattern of pressure cells that would exist for a land-free world.

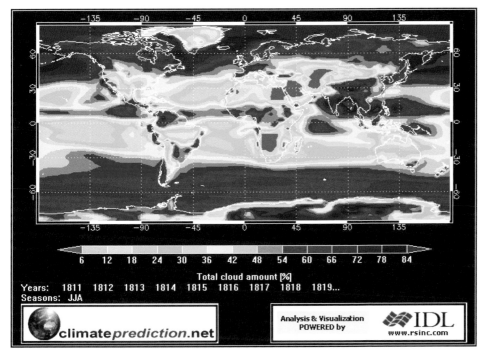

Figure 6.8 Modelled global cloud cover during June, July and August.

- Looking again at Figure 6.8, you can see that the ITCZ is not on the Equator but north of it. Similarly, the cloud band in the mid-latitudes in the Southern Hemisphere is between 60° S and 30° S, instead of being centred on 60° S. Why do you think this is?

- This map is an average for the months June, July and August when the Northern Hemisphere is experiencing summer and the Sun is overhead at noon, not at the Equator but north of it. On 21 June the Sun is overhead at latitude 23.4° N (Figure 3.14). Because the latitude of maximum heating, and hence the ITCZ, is shifted north, so too is the junction of the polar and Ferrel cells.

6.3.2 Cyclonic and anticyclonic air flow

The Coriolis effect increases with increasing latitude. This is because the speed at which the Earth's surface rotates decreases only slightly with increasing latitude near the Equator but more quickly nearer the poles. This causes a change in the style of atmospheric circulation with latitude. The Trade Winds, which blow in tropical latitudes where the Coriolis effect is relatively small, are deflected laterally only slightly and the overall pattern of circulation is the predominantly vertical Hadley circulation. At higher latitudes, where the degree of deflection is much greater, vortices tend to form in the lower atmosphere and have a predominantly horizontal, or slanting, circulation. These are the anticyclonic and cyclonic winds familiar from weather charts, as shown in Figure 6.9.

You may recall from Section 5.1 that pressure is a measure of the force exerted by particles colliding with a surface area (Figure 5.4 and equation 5.1). Consequently, winds generally blow from regions of high pressure (high force) to regions of low pressure (low force). The Coriolis force deflects wind flow to the right in the Northern Hemisphere, so winds flowing outwards from a high-pressure region in the Northern Hemisphere flow clockwise. The same effect in the Southern Hemisphere makes them flow anticlockwise around high-pressure regions. Flows associated with high-pressure systems are referred to as anticyclonic. Winds blowing in the opposite direction around low-pressure regions are referred to as cyclonic. The outward, anticyclonic flow from a high-pressure system is associated with a descending column of air, while the inward, cyclonic flow from a low-pressure system is accompanied by rising air (Figure 6.9).

The phenomena we have discussed so far are the normal high and low pressure systems which move energy around in the atmosphere every day. In low latitudes over warm oceans, large-scale evaporation and convection lead to the development of intense low-pressure systems and clusters of thunderstorms. Condensation from wet rising air liberates latent heat that intensifies the convection even further. If this kind of system develops far enough away from the Equator for the Coriolis effect to be significant (usually greater than 5° north or south), the whole mass of air begins to rotate cyclonically. As the system moves poleward, the increasing Coriolis effect makes the mass spin faster. Provided it stays over a source of warmth and moisture (i.e. over warm oceans), latent heat and convection continue to fuel the system. When wind speeds reach 62 kilometres per hour (km h^{-1}), the system is referred to as a tropical storm.

Figure 6.9 (a) Air spiralling downwards and outwards from an atmospheric high (an anticyclone). (b) Air spiralling inwards and upwards towards an atmospheric low (a cyclone or depression). The flow directions shown are for the Northern Hemisphere; in the Southern Hemisphere the flow around anticyclones is anticlockwise and the flow around cyclones is clockwise. Contour values are typical atmospheric pressures at sea-level, expressed in millibars. Surface wind speeds typically reach a few tens of metres per second.

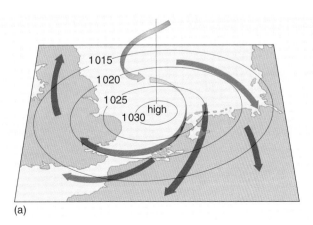

(a)

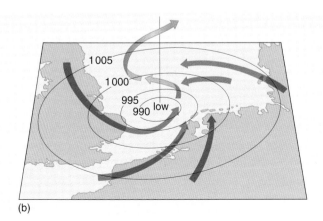

(b)

At 119 km h^{-1} the storm is reclassified as a hurricane, typhoon or cyclone, depending on its location. They are hurricanes if they occur in the eastern Pacific and Atlantic Oceans; typhoons if they occur west of the international dateline (180° longitude); and tropical cyclones if they occur in the Indian Ocean and around Australia. Figure 6.10 shows such a system.

Atmospheric pressures associated with these systems can be less than 920 mb and such lows can locally raise sea-levels by as much as 5 to 6 metres. (Think of normal atmospheric pressure being the force of the weight of the atmosphere pushing down on the surface area of the sea. If the pressure is reduced, the sea will rebound slightly.) When such systems approach coastal regions this storm surge causes widespread flooding. However, when over land, hurricanes, typhoons and cyclones quickly lose energy and dissipate because they are denied the moisture and hence latent heat release that is required to fuel their convective motion.

● Would the number of tropical storms change if the climate changes?

◍ Tropical storms rely on the energy released by the evaporation and condensation of water from the warm ocean surface. It is therefore reasonable to expect that, the warmer the surface of the ocean, the greater the number of storms. However, forecasting individual, intense low-pressure systems is notoriously difficult because many different factors can affect them.

Figure 6.10 Typhoon Lupit, over the Philippine Sea in November 2003, had winds estimated at more than 260 km h^{-1}. The main part of the typhoon is nearly 1300 km wide.

6.3.3 Large scale-atmospheric mixing and heat transport

We have seen that the large-scale circulation patterns – the Hadley, Ferrel and polar cells – transport energy from equatorial regions towards the poles. However, small-scale features such as cyclones and anticyclones are responsible for much more of the poleward transport of heat in the Earth's atmosphere.

● How do you think mid-latitude cyclones and anticyclones contribute to the poleward transport of heat?

◍ Air moving northwards in a Northern Hemisphere cyclone or anticyclone will transport relatively warm air poleward, where it mixes with adjacent air masses along atmospheric fronts, and heat is exchanged between them. This, in effect, is a large-scale stirring of the atmosphere.

The paths taken by mid-latitude depressions and anticyclones are determined by the behaviour of the polar jet stream, which is a high-speed, eastward-flowing air current encircling the globe in each hemisphere at altitudes of approximately 10 km. It lies above the boundary between warm tropical air and the underlying cold polar air, known as the polar front. The jet stream tends to develop large undulations or waves, typically three to six of them around the globe, which eventually become so extreme that cells of tropical air become isolated at relatively high latitudes, and cells of polar air become isolated at relatively low latitudes, as shown in Figure 6.11.

This mechanism results in the horizontal transport of enormous masses of warm air poleward and cold air towards the Equator. Meanwhile, vertical air movements that accompany these large-scale horizontal wave motions lead to the

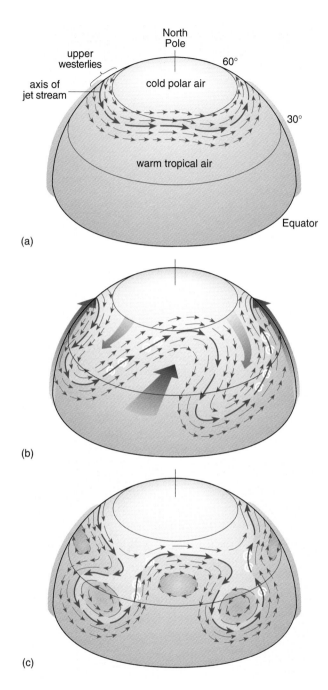

(a)

(b)

(c)

Figure 6.11 (above)
Schematic diagram showing
stages in the development of
waves in the northern polar jet
stream: (a) the jet stream begins
to undulate; (b) the waves
become more extreme;
(c) large cells of cold polar
and warm tropical air
become isolated.

development of cyclonic flow and low-pressure centres,
and anticyclonic flow and high-pressure centres, near the
Earth's surface.

● What would be the effect of the undulations in the jet
stream becoming more pronounced?

◉ More cold polar air will flow to lower latitudes than
normal, while more warm tropical air will flow to higher
latitudes than normal. This would increase the transport
of energy towards the poles.

Figure 6.5 shows, for the idealised ocean world, that the
latitudes of 30° N and S, where the Hadley cells descend,
are characterised by high-pressure systems called the
subtropical highs, while latitudes of 60° N and S, where the
polar cells ascend, are characterised by low-pressure
systems called the subpolar lows. Between these systems
westerly (i.e. eastward flowing) winds prevail which,
depending on the configuration of the polar jet stream, may
be affected by cold polar air or warm tropical air. These
regions are often called temperate. In contrast to that view
for an idealised ocean world, Figure 6.12 (opposite) shows
the prevailing winds that are actually observed at the
Earth's surface.

● Over which parts of the globe are the subtropical highs
and subpolar lows most evident?

◉ Subpolar lows and subtropical highs are most evident in
Figure 6.12 over the oceans, which is not surprising
given that their appearance in Figure 6.5 was
appropriate to an Earth completely covered in water.

● By comparing the wind patterns in Figure 6.12 with
those in Figure 6.5, can you say which features of the
real world cause the actual wind pattern to differ from
the hypothetical one shown in Figure 6.5?

◉ Following on from the previous question, it is the
presence of the continental land masses that makes
the real wind pattern so much more complicated in
Figure 6.12.

Figure 6.12 (right) The observed (as distinct from model-generated) prevailing
winds at the Earth's surface, and the position of the ITCZ where the wind
systems of the two hemispheres meet, in (a) July (northern summer/southern
winter) and (b) January (southern summer/northern winter). Also shown are the
positions of the main regions of high atmospheric pressure (red/pink tones) in the
tropics, and low atmospheric pressure (blue tones) at low latitudes and in
subpolar regions, at those seasons of the year.

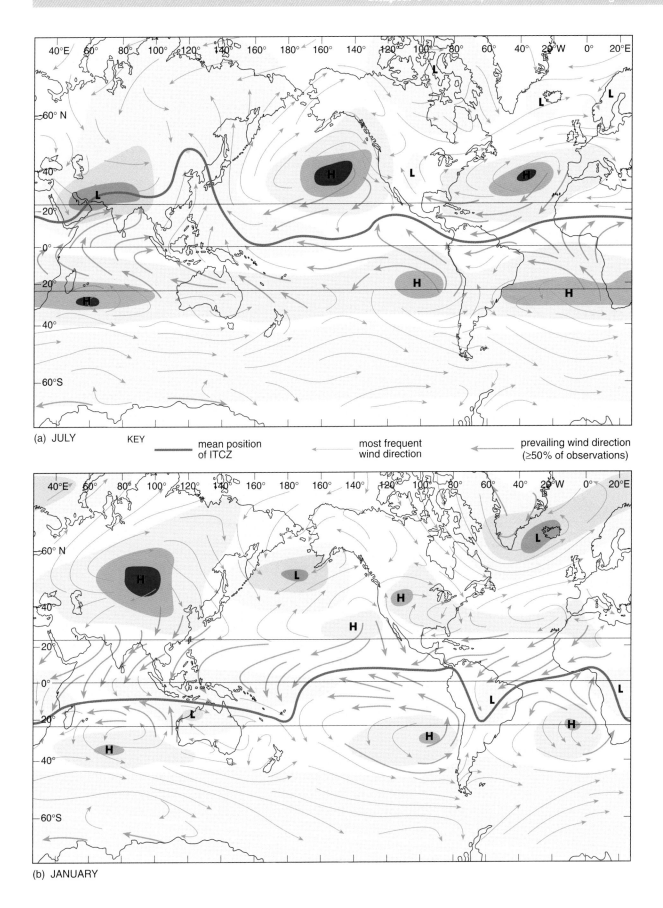

(a) JULY   KEY ——— mean position of ITCZ   ←— most frequent wind direction   ⇐ prevailing wind direction (≥50% of observations)

(b) JANUARY

So, the presence of the continents distorts the global wind system from hypothetical zones of polar high/subpolar low/subtropical high/equatorial low. It is clear, therefore, that weather and climate models require realistic representations of global land-forms in order to predict circulation (and energy transport) patterns correctly.

To discover more about the effects of the distribution of land and ocean, try answering the following questions.

● The ITCZ, where the wind systems of the two hemispheres meet (Figure 6.12), generally follows the zone of highest temperature at the Earth's surface. In general terms, what are the main differences between the position and/or shape of the ITCZ in July (Figure 6.12a) and January (Figure 6.12b)?

● First, the ITCZ is (mostly) further north in July and further south in January; in other words, it shifts into the hemisphere experiencing summer, particularly over large land masses. This is what we would expect because the ITCZ – an area of vigorous upward convection and hence cloud generation – tends to be located over the warmest parts of the Earth's surface. We saw this effect in a climate model in Figure 6.8.

● The ITCZ moves seasonally northwards and southwards between the extreme positions shown in Figure 6.12. What implication does the changing position of the ITCZ have for the prevailing wind direction at the Earth's surface? To answer this, describe how the wind direction changes over tropical West Africa between July and January.

● In July, when the ITCZ is at its most northerly, the winds over tropical West Africa are mainly southerly (i.e. from the south). In January, when the ITCZ is at its most southerly, the winds over the region are mainly easterly or northeasterly (i.e. from the east or northeast). Such seasonally reversing winds produce the monsoons, which are discussed further below.

● Over which region is the north–south seasonal shift in the position of the ITCZ greatest?

● The north–south shift in the position of the ITCZ is most marked over the northern Indian Ocean and over the western tropical Pacific and South East Asia.

Many low-latitude regions experience seasonal reversals in wind direction when the ITCZ moves across them from north to south or vice versa. Air masses that travel over the oceans pick up moisture, and those that move over arid regions are dry, so seasonally reversing winds often bring with them contrasting climatic conditions (Figure 6.13). If the ITCZ moves over the land while it is drawing in moist air from over the ocean, monsoon conditions result. In Figure 6.12, for example, the air flow over India in January is from the north and dry continental air flows in. However, in July the ITCZ lies just to the north of India and the prevailing wind carries in moist air from across the Indian Ocean. The strong convection set up at the ITCZ leads to a band of heavy precipitation across India – the monsoon. This accounts for the period of extremely heavy rain which is experienced in New Delhi for just a few months in the middle of each year, while at other times of the year the New Delhi climate is much drier (Figure 5.15).

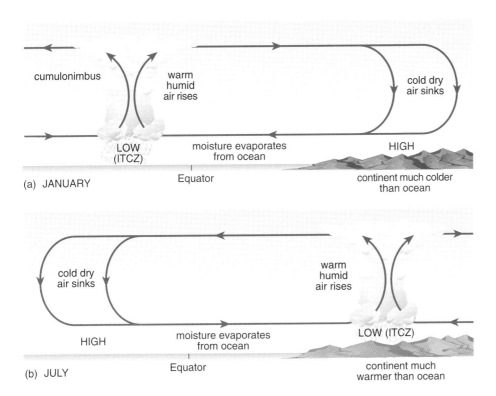

Figure 6.13 The changing conditions over continent and ocean in a monsoon climate, assuming that the continent is in the Northern Hemisphere. (a) Northern winter: dry cooled air subsides over the continent while warm moist air rises at the ITCZ, causing abundant rain over the ocean. (b) Northern summer: the land is now much warmer than the ocean, so the ITCZ and its zone of rain has moved northwards over the continent.

- Bearing in mind these seasonal reversals in wind direction, how might you expect conditions in South East Asia to differ between July and January?

- Conditions will be wet in July, when the prevailing winds are southwesterlies blowing off the Indian Ocean, and dry in January, when the prevailing winds are northeasterlies blowing off the Eurasian continent.

In Section 5.3.2, we saw how the interaction between prevailing winds and topographical features such as mountains can influence the local climate by producing orographic precipitation on the windward side of mountain ranges and a rain shadow in their lee. The most extreme example of this affects the climate over a huge area of Asia, and resembles the monsoon in some ways. It is caused by the largest and highest land mass on Earth: the Tibetan Plateau at about 30° N and 90° E. At an average altitude of 5000 m, the air above Tibet is relatively thin and solar radiation absorbed by the surface in the summer heats the air above it to a much greater extent than air at that altitude would normally be heated. This heated air rises, creating a strong low-pressure cell that draws in air from around it. Warm moist air from over the Indian Ocean is forced to rise as it encounters the flanks of the plateau and, in particular, the Himalayan mountains. This rising air expands, cools and the moisture precipitates as intense rain. In winter the Tibetan Plateau cools down more than the surrounding areas and a high-pressure region develops, reversing the air flow and bringing dry weather over the surrounding region.

Our discussion of large-scale heat transport has concentrated on the atmosphere but oceans are equally important. The atmosphere and the oceans are each responsible for about 50% of the heat transfer from the tropics to the mid-latitude and polar regions. Most of the heat transferred by the atmosphere is associated with small-scale low-pressure and high-pressure systems rather than the large-scale Hadley circulation of the atmosphere.

We have now seen how the vertical transport of energy in the atmosphere, which is brought about by convection, is complemented by horizontal transport in circulation currents, moderated by the Coriolis effect. In Chapter 7 we shall look in more detail at the particles that make up the atmosphere, and at how the shape of something as small as a molecule can affect the climate at the Earth's surface.

6.4   Summary of Chapter 6

1   The large-scale and small-scale movement of air and water around the Earth advects and redistributes heat.

2   Many of the circulation patterns in the atmosphere are determined principally by the Coriolis effect.

3   All of the large-scale weather patterns, such as the jet stream and the Asian monsoon, vary with time – both seasonally and on longer time-scales. As the climate changes, so do these phenomena.

7 Atmospheric carbon dioxide and other gases

'We live inside a blue chamber, a bubble of air blown by ourselves.'
Lewis Thomas

At the end of Chapter 4 we introduced the greenhouse effect, which is caused by the presence of 'greenhouse gases' in the atmosphere. In this chapter we look at what makes a gas a greenhouse gas and how the amount of carbon dioxide in the atmosphere can change through the carbon cycle.

7.1 Atoms and molecules

In Chapter 5 we saw that, by considering a gas as being comprised of particles, we could explain how the processes of conduction, convection and latent heat transfer affect the temperature of the atmosphere. We are close to completing our study of the effect of the atmosphere on the Earth's surface temperature, but we now need to consider in more detail the nature of the particles – the fact that they are atoms and molecules.

7.1.1 Describing atoms and molecules

All ordinary matter is composed of atoms, which for the moment we can visualise as hard spheres. They are very small, roughly 10^{-10} m across. Although all matter is made of atoms, not all atoms are the same. There are 100 or so different types of atom, including oxygen atoms, nitrogen atoms, carbon atoms, hydrogen atoms, argon atoms and iron atoms, which give us the basic building blocks from which everything in the world is made. Using different atoms, or joining them in different ways, produces, for example, water, salt, glass or a tree – or any other substance you can name in the whole Universe!

Atoms are the smallest chemical entities of substances known as chemical elements, or elements for short, each of which consists of just one type of atom. Hence there are 100 or so different elements, which cannot be converted into another element by chemical reactions.

Molecules are formed when two or more atoms bond together. Many of the gases that make up the Earth's atmosphere are molecules rather than atoms. The major constituents of the atmosphere are shown in Table 7.1. The other components are present only in trace amounts.

Table 7.1 The gaseous composition of the Earth's atmosphere at sea-level (main components only).

Component	No. of molecules or atoms as % of total number	No. of molecules or atoms in a cubic metre	Mass as % of total mass
nitrogen	77.6	2.0×10^{25}	75.5
oxygen	20.9	5.4×10^{24}	23.2
argon	0.93	2.4×10^{23}	1.28
water[*]	0.5	1.3×10^{23}	0.3
carbon dioxide[**]	3.7×10^{-2}	9.2×10^{21}	5.3×10^{-2}

[*] Highly variable, so average values are given. [**] Increasing annually: this is the 2002 figure.

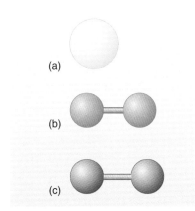

Figure 7.1 Three of the gaseous elements in air, shown as a 'ball-and-stick' representation. Argon (a) exists as single atoms but nitrogen (b) and oxygen (c) both exist as pairs of atoms. Pale blue, dark blue and red are used here to distinguish the atoms of argon, nitrogen and oxygen, respectively.

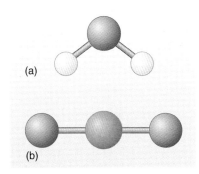

Figure 7.2 Ball-and-stick diagrams of: (a) a water molecule – oxygen and hydrogen atoms are represented by red and white balls, respectively; (b) a carbon dioxide molecule – carbon and oxygen atoms are represented by black and red balls, respectively. Water is often written in the shorthand form H_2O, pronounced 'aitch two oh'. This is because a molecule of water contains two **H**ydrogen atoms and one **O**xygen atom. Similarly, carbon dioxide is often written as CO_2, pronounced 'see oh two'.

- What are the two main components of the atmosphere?

- Table 7.1 shows that by far the largest component is nitrogen, followed by oxygen.

Only one of the gases in Table 7.1 – argon – exists as single atoms, represented by a pale blue sphere in Figure 7.1a. The smallest particle of each of the other gaseous elements in Table 7.1 is a molecule. Thus, the main atmospheric constituent – nitrogen – does not exist as single atoms but as nitrogen atoms bonded together in pairs, which can be represented as shown in Figure 7.1b. Similarly, oxygen in the air exists as pairs of oxygen atoms that form a molecule, as shown in Figure 7.1c. The relative numbers of each type of molecule (atoms in the case of argon) in Table 7.1 show that the air consists almost entirely of nitrogen molecules and oxygen molecules, with smaller numbers of argon atoms, water molecules and carbon dioxide molecules. In Table 7.1 the percentage composition based on the number of particles (atoms or molecules) differs from the percentage composition by mass because the different types of atom have different masses.

The images in Figure 7.1 are 'ball-and-stick' representations in which atoms are shown as hard spheres or 'balls'; different colours are used to distinguish the various types of atom; and each bond in a molecule is represented by a 'stick' between the two atoms involved (Figure 7.1b and c), indicating the forces holding the molecule together.

Chemical compounds are molecules built up from more than one type of atom. Most of the substances in the world around you fall into this category, as do two of the main atmospheric constituents – water and carbon dioxide. Each water molecule is constructed from one oxygen atom and two hydrogen atoms joined together, as in Figure 7.2a. This figure shows that water is a chemical compound in which the oxygen atom is bonded to both of the hydrogen atoms so that the molecule is bent, i.e. the three atoms are not arranged in a straight line.

- What can you say about the carbon dioxide molecule shown in Figure 7.2b?

- Carbon dioxide is a chemical compound containing one carbon atom and two oxygen atoms. The carbon atom is bonded to both of the oxygen atoms so that the molecule is linear, not bent like the water molecule.

Figure 7.3 shows a representation of methane – a trace constituent of the atmosphere. Here, as in the water molecule, the bonds do *not* lie in one plane: Figure 7.3 is actually a two-dimensional drawing of a three-dimensional structure.

- Which elements are present in methane and how many atoms of each element are there in a molecule of methane? How many bonds are there, and which atoms do the bonds join together?

- Figure 7.3 shows that each molecule of methane contains one carbon atom and four hydrogen atoms. There are four bonds, each between the carbon atom and a hydrogen atom.

The important general point about the examples in Figures 7.1, 7.2 and 7.3 is that real molecules are constructed from certain atoms, which are held together by a specific number of bonds and are arranged relative to one another in space in a particular way.

7.1.2 **Combustion and respiration reactions**

Having learned a little about the molecular make-up of the most common gases in the atmosphere, we now take a brief look at some of their properties when they interact. We shall concentrate on those aspects that are most important for their effect on climate. For this reason we shall not consider nitrogen and argon because they are relatively or completely unreactive.

One key property of oxygen is its chemical reactivity. Given the right circumstances, it can combine with many other elements to form chemical compounds. For example, coal is mostly made up of rather complicated molecules which contain mainly carbon atoms. When we burn coal, carbon atoms in the coal combine with oxygen atoms from the oxygen molecules in the air to form carbon dioxide molecules. We can write this chemical reaction simply as:

oxygen and carbon react to form carbon dioxide [7.1]

In this chemical reaction, the carbon and oxygen are referred to as the reactants and carbon dioxide as the product.

Coal is called a fossil fuel because it is made up of the remains of ancient organisms (in the case of coal, those organisms are plants) which, like us, were made substantially of carbon-bearing molecules. Complex molecules containing carbon are also referred to as organic compounds. When those organisms died some of the carbon was buried in sediments that, over time, turned into rock. The form in which that ancient carbon survives (mostly coal, oil or gas) depends on its original composition, the depth it was buried and the length of time it was buried. Because fossil fuels are rich in both carbon and hydrogen, we also refer to them as hydrocarbons. As you will see in Section 7.4, the burning of fossil fuels has an important effect on the GMST.

Natural gas is a fossil fuel consisting mainly of methane, whose structure you saw in Figure 7.3. We can express the burning of methane in air as:

oxygen and methane react to form water and carbon dioxide [7.2]

The molecules involved in this chemical reaction are shown in Figure 7.4.

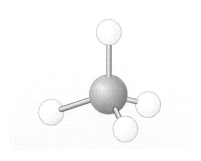

Figure 7.3 The structure of methane. The colour code is the same as in Figures 7.1 and 7.2.

- According to Figure 7.4, how many atoms of carbon, oxygen and hydrogen are there in the reactants – methane and oxygen – and in the products – carbon dioxide and water?

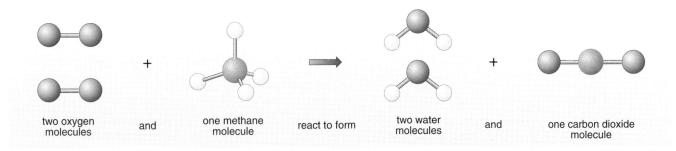

two oxygen molecules and one methane molecule react to form two water molecules and one carbon dioxide molecule

Figure 7.4 The molecules involved in the reaction between oxygen and methane. The colour code is the same as in the previous figures.

◈ Figure 7.4 shows that one molecule of methane reacts with two molecules of oxygen. Thus the reactants contain one carbon atom, four hydrogen atoms and four oxygen atoms. The products are one molecule of carbon dioxide and two molecules of water, which also contain one carbon atom, four hydrogen atoms and four oxygen atoms.

Note that we have the same number of atoms of each element in the reactants as in the products. During a chemical reaction, atoms are neither created nor destroyed. Instead, existing bonds are broken, new bonds are made, and the atoms exchange their partners. For example, in Figure 7.4 the hydrogen atoms are bonded to a carbon atom in the reactants but to oxygen atoms in the products.

● Will carbon react with oxygen to form water?

◈ No. Water molecules contain hydrogen atoms (Figure 7.4), thus water will never be one product of a reaction between the elements carbon and oxygen.

We burn fossil fuels to obtain energy. The energy is released as a result of the reaction between the fuel and oxygen in the air, so we can extend our description:

oxygen and hydrocarbon fuel react to form water and carbon dioxide, and energy is released   [7.3]

Note that the fuel is not converted in some way into energy. The hydrocarbon fuel reacts with oxygen in the air to give carbon dioxide and water. The energy released comes from the breaking and making of chemical bonds. When bonds are broken an input of energy is required. When bonds are formed between atoms energy is released. So, if in a chemical reaction the released energy (from making bonds) is greater than the input of energy (for breaking bonds), the reaction as a whole gives out energy, usually as kinetic energy (i.e. the energy associated with motion that you met in Section 2.1). As a result, the temperature rises.

Oxygen plays an identical role in sustaining all animal life. When we breathe, we draw in air and absorb some of the oxygen into our bloodstream, which carries it around the body. Just as with fossil fuels, oxygen reacts with substances in the body to give water and carbon dioxide, and energy is released. The carbon dioxide is exhaled. This reaction between oxygen and carbon-rich substances in an animal's body, to release energy to drive life processes and producing carbon dioxide, is called respiration. We shall look further at respiration and its counterpart in plants – photosynthesis – in Section 7.3. Respiration is an important process in the carbon cycle, which is described in more detail in Section 7.3. Basically, it transforms carbon which is also locked up in organic matter – the food that animals eat – into carbon dioxide in the atmosphere.

You have seen, from the various reactions described above, that water and carbon dioxide are produced when fossil fuels are burned in air as well as being produced by all living organisms in the process of respiration. Neither water nor carbon dioxide reacts particularly well with any of the other atmospheric gases although, as you will see in Section 7.2, they are both greenhouse gases and therefore crucial for life on Earth.

- The reaction between petrol, which is refined from oil, and oxygen provides the energy to move a car. Oxygen is supplied through the air intake and petrol is provided from the fuel tank. What is expelled from the exhaust?

- Petrol, being derived from a fossil fuel, consists of hydrocarbon molecules. It reacts with oxygen to give carbon dioxide and water. These exit from the engine through the exhaust. This reaction gives out energy that is used to move the car (reaction 7.3).

Many people believe that petrol is in some way converted into energy and only a little waste material exits from the exhaust. In fact, under ideal combustion conditions, one litre of petrol (about 1 kg) reacts with about 4 kg of oxygen from the air to produce 5 kg of waste gas, consisting of 3.5 kg of carbon dioxide and 1.5 kg of water, which escape through the exhaust. (In less than ideal conditions, other products regarded as pollutants are produced as well. Catalytic converters remove some of these pollutants.)

As you will see in Section 7.4, changes to the amount of carbon dioxide in the atmosphere are a matter of concern. The taxation of motor vehicles in the UK is now related to the amount of carbon dioxide produced per kilometre driven, and international agreements, such as the Kyoto protocol, seek to limit the amount of carbon dioxide a country emits into the atmosphere.

7.2 The greenhouse gases

In Section 7.1 we saw what the major constituents of the atmosphere are, what their molecular structures are, and how they are consumed or produced in combustion and respiration reactions. In this section we shall consider which features of certain gases, most importantly water vapour and carbon dioxide, make them greenhouse gases.

To begin, look again at Figure 4.9 and recall that one of the important mechanisms by which energy is transferred to and from the atmosphere is the absorption and emission of radiation.

- What happens when the Earth's surface absorbs either solar radiation or infrared radiation emitted by the atmosphere?

- In both cases, the absorption of radiation leads to an input of energy to the Earth's surface. By itself, this would lead to an increase in the surface temperature.

- Which type of radiation is strongly absorbed by the Earth's atmosphere, and why is this important for the GMST?

- The atmosphere is a strong absorber of longwave infrared radiation and thus captures and recycles most of the radiation emitted by the Earth's surface. If this were not the case, there would be no greenhouse effect and the Earth's surface would be about 35 °C cooler than it actually is.

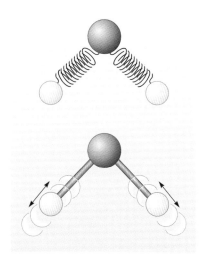

Figure 7.5 A water molecule where the bonds are represented as springs. The double-headed arrows show that the bond can vibrate.

Although we used a 'ball-and-stick' representation of molecules in Section 7.1, the chemical bonds that hold molecules together are more like springs than sticks: they can vibrate, as shown in Figure 7.5 for water. When the bond (or spring) absorbs energy from infrared radiation, it vibrates more energetically. However, as we hinted towards the end of Chapter 4, only certain gases in the atmosphere actually absorb infrared radiation. For reasons that are too complicated go into here, infrared radiation is absorbed only if a molecule contains more than two atoms or, if it contains only two atoms, the atoms at each end of the bond are of different elements.

● Which of the atmospheric constituents in Table 7.1 can absorb infrared radiation through changes in their vibration? (Figures 7.1 and 7.2 will help you.)

◐ Argon exists as single atoms, so there are no bonds and it will not absorb infrared radiation. Oxygen and nitrogen molecules consist of two atoms of the same element attached by a bond (Figure 7.1), so these molecules will not absorb infrared radiation. Molecules of carbon dioxide and water both contain more than two atoms (Figure 7.2), so these compounds will absorb infrared radiation through changes in how their bonds vibrate.

A molecule can absorb infrared radiation in a second way, by rotation of the molecule. If infrared radiation is absorbed, the molecule will rotate faster. Of the atmospheric gases listed in Table 7.1, only water can absorb infrared radiation in this way.

We can conclude that nitrogen, oxygen and argon will not behave as greenhouse gases but, because water vapour and carbon dioxide can absorb infrared radiation, they are greenhouse gases. Although they are two minor components of the atmosphere (see Table 7.1), carbon dioxide (0.036% by number) and water vapour (0.5%) cause most of the considerable increase in the GMST attributed to the greenhouse effect. The larger contribution (about 60%) is made by water vapour.

The amounts of these two gases in the atmosphere are very important. The amount of infrared radiation absorbed depends on how many water and carbon dioxide molecules are present in the atmosphere: the more molecules present, the greater the proportion of radiation absorbed.

● Look again at Figure 4.9 and consider what would happen if there were *less* water vapour and carbon dioxide in the atmosphere.

◐ We might predict that less of the outgoing infrared radiation would be absorbed and more would escape directly to space. The atmosphere would then emit less radiation because less had been absorbed. This would lead to a reduction in the amount of radiation absorbed by the Earth's surface. This alone would result in a lower GMST. Thus, the greenhouse effect would be reduced.

We can also suggest that if there were more carbon dioxide and water vapour in the atmosphere, more infrared radiation would be absorbed and thus more would be emitted, so the greenhouse effect would be greater – the GMST would be higher.

We considered the factors that affect the amount of water vapour in the atmosphere as part of the water cycle in Chapter 5. We now need to consider the carbon cycle, so that we can see what controls the amount of carbon dioxide (CO_2) in the atmosphere.

7.3 The carbon cycle

Although the amount of CO_2 in the atmosphere can easily be measured, we cannot say from such measurements whether that amount might change over time: either in the short term (days, months or years) or the long term (thousands or millions of years). To do that, we must understand what controls the release of CO_2 to the atmosphere from other carbon reservoirs and what controls the removal of CO_2 from the atmosphere into other carbon reservoirs. Without some understanding of the entire carbon cycle, therefore, we cannot predict how the continued release of CO_2 into the atmosphere from burning fossil fuels may change the Earth's climate.

The global carbon cycle describes the movement and major transformations of carbon on Earth and, just like the water cycle in Figure 5.19, it can be divided into a series of 'reservoirs' in which carbon resides. However, unlike the water cycle, where water remains as a single compound throughout the cycle, merely changing state, in the carbon cycle the element carbon appears in numerous forms, a tiny sample of which was mentioned in Section 7.1.2 (e.g. CO_2, organic compounds and methane).

The key to understanding the carbon cycle, as with any cycle, is to recognise that the various reservoirs do not exist in isolation; rather, carbon is constantly transferred among them. Carbon moves rapidly through some reservoirs while in others its residence time is very long (thousands or millions of years). Changes in one reservoir (e.g. through burning fossil fuels) can have important effects elsewhere in the cycle, although it may not be obvious exactly what those effects are.

The global carbon cycle has numerous reservoirs, some with residence times of years to tens of years, and others where the time-scales are thousands to millions of years. To simplify this, in this section we look only at the subset of reservoirs that most affect the atmospheric CO_2 concentration, and the processes by which they absorb or release CO_2. We need to consider four key reservoirs: the atmosphere itself, which is a reservoir of CO_2; biomass, which is a reservoir of organic compounds; soil and detritus, which likewise is a reservoir of organic compounds; and preserved organic carbon, since that includes the fossil fuels. The flows between these four reservoirs are summarised in Figure 7.6. As we have already discussed the atmosphere earlier in this chapter, we shall discuss only the other three key reservoirs below.

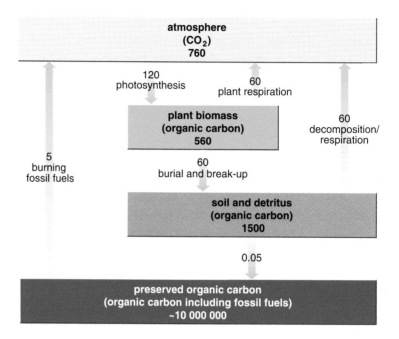

Figure 7.6 The four main reservoirs of the carbon cycle that are key to the atmospheric CO_2 concentration. The approximate mass of each reservoir is given in units of 10^{12} kilograms of carbon (kg C) and the flow rates between reservoirs are given in units of 10^{12} kg C y^{-1}.

7.3.1 Biomass

Organic matter (plants, animals and micro-organisms) is composed principally of carbon-bearing molecules, and most of that carbon is in vegetation. The total mass of organisms is called the biomass, which is usually expressed either as the mass of dry material (kg) or the mass of carbon (kg C) contained in that dry material. This reservoir of carbon is very unevenly spread over the Earth's surface. For example, there is more than 100 times as much biomass on land (mainly trees) as there is in the ocean (mainly micro-organisms and seaweed). (The ocean biomass is not included in Figure 7.6.)

Estimating the total biomass of the Earth is notoriously difficult, largely because of the difficulty of calculating the biomass of tropical forests. Scientists' best guess of the global biomass is currently about 560×10^{12} kg of carbon (abbreviated to kg C). This is an enormous mass but it is spread over the Earth's surface and averages out to about 4 kg of carbon per square metre (4 kg C m^{-2}) on land. Animals (including humans) account for less than 0.2% of the total: the rest is stored in plants.

- A good-sized bush contains roughly 4 kg C. Which areas of the world might contain more plant material in an average square metre and therefore more total carbon stored in plant biomass? Which areas might contain less?

◉ Areas such as forests or swamps might contain more plant biomass and therefore more carbon per square metre. Very cold or very dry areas of the Earth have little vegetation and would contain less than 4 kg C m^{-2}.

The smallest amounts of biomass per square metre on the Earth's land surface (<0.3 kg C m^{-2}) are in lakes and streams, polar regions, tundra and deserts (see Figure 1.4). On the other hand, tropical rainforests support an astonishing 20 kg C m^{-2}. In comparison, agricultural land supports roughly 0.5 kg C m^{-2}.

● In terms of global biomass, what would be the net result of converting large areas of tropical rainforest into agricultural land?

◉ The conversion of tropical rainforest into agricultural land means that less carbon is stored globally in biomass. Therefore, some other reservoir(s) will gain carbon. Deforestation can lead, in part, to an increase in atmospheric CO_2.

Replanting trees after a forest is cut down does not immediately compensate for the loss of the mature forest because, until the trees are mature, the land is effectively like that used for agriculture. To achieve the high carbon-storage capacity of a tropical rainforest, the trees must be mature and all possible parts of the forest structure must be filled with appropriately adapted photosynthesising plants, their pollinators and seed-dispersal agents.

Photosynthesis is the process by which green plants make organic matter from water and carbon dioxide, using the energy from solar radiation. The process is also the source of most of the oxygen in the atmosphere and the basis for the existence of virtually all forms of life. Photosynthesis can be summarised as:

$CO_2 + H_2O$ and solar energy gives O_2 and organic compounds (sugars) **[7.4]**

CO_2 is taken into the plant from the air, through specialised pores called stomata, which are mostly on the undersides of the leaves. In contrast, the water is drawn in through the roots and is transported to leaves where solar radiation facilitates the reaction. You should be aware, however, that this summary gives only the overall result: photosynthesis requires many steps, and many complex intermediate chemical compounds are formed.

Other than a few minerals, all of the material that makes a green plant or a tree comes either from the atmosphere (CO_2) or from rain (H_2O).

The important general point for the carbon cycle is that green plants move carbon from the atmosphere reservoir as CO_2 into the biomass reservoir as organic molecules by the process of photosynthesis.

Some of the carbon removed from the atmosphere by plants as CO_2 is returned by both plants and animals through respiration. Respiration encompasses the chemical reactions by which an organism breaks down simple organic compounds to release energy. Plants use the energy released by respiration in maintenance, reproduction and the growth of plant tissue. The net effect can be expressed in the chemical reaction:

organic carbon and O_2 react to form CO_2 and H_2O, and energy is released **[7.5]**

Compare this respiration reaction with reaction 7.3, which describes the burning of fossil fuel (Section 7.1.2). You should see that they are nearly identical – only here we have substituted 'organic carbon' for 'hydrocarbon fuel'. In fact, the two chemical reactions are really no different, since fossil fuel (oil, coal and natural gas) is a form of organic carbon.

Now, compare the chemical reaction for respiration (7.5) with that for photosynthesis (7.4). You can see that respiration is essentially the reverse of photosynthesis: instead of energy, water and carbon dioxide being used to grow plant tissue and produce oxygen, plant tissue is broken down when it reacts with oxygen to yield carbon dioxide, water and energy. Plants acquire energy by breaking down the simple organic compounds (sugars) they have made by photosynthesis. Some animals, such as bees, slugs and panda bears, acquire energy by eating parts of plants; others, such as lions and killer whales, by eating other animals. In all cases, energy is obtained from the organic compounds in the food and carbon dioxide is released into the atmosphere.

Studies estimate that approximately 120×10^{12} kg C y^{-1} is taken into plant biomass through photosynthesis and about half of that (60×10^{12} kg C y^{-1}) is released back into the atmosphere through plant respiration (Figure 7.6).

● Where does the rest go?

◉ The remaining 60×10^{12} kg C y^{-1} is incorporated into plant tissue.

Most of this carbon goes into building new tissue such as leaves, flowers and seeds; a much smaller amount goes into producing more 'permanent' plant tissue (e.g. wood, branches and bark) in long-lived species. About 5 to 10% is consumed by animals, thus directly (animals eating plants) or indirectly (animals eating animals) supporting nearly all the animal life on Earth.

7.3.2 Soil and detritus

Nearly all of the 60×10^{12} kg C y^{-1} stored by plants as plant tissue eventually goes into the soil. Soil is the mixture of minerals and organic material occurring above bedrock on the Earth's (land) surface. Most of the transfer of carbon from the plant biomass reservoir to the soil and detritus reservoir occurs when seasonal vegetation dies or sheds its leaves. However, this transfer also includes the death of long-lived plant species and animals which eat the plants.

The transfer rate of 60×10^{12} kg C y^{-1} from living organisms to soil is equivalent to about 3 to 4 kg of fresh plant material (not just carbon) deposited over each square metre on the Earth's land surface each year. However, much of this material breaks up and subsequently decomposes. Decomposition is simply another word for the respiration of organisms such as worms, beetles, fungi and bacteria, which use the organic compounds in dead organic matter to provide energy:

organic carbon and O_2 react to form CO_2 and H_2O, and energy is released   **[7.6]**

Chemically, the results of the processes of decomposition, respiration and burning are the same – note the similarities of reactions 7.6, 7.5 and 7.3.

Oxygen-breathing decomposer organisms can live only where there is an abundant supply of oxygen. In areas where very little oxygen penetrates, such as marshes and bogs, respiration and decomposition are slowed down, and organic matter gradually accumulates. We shall explore the consequences of this for the global carbon cycle in Section 7.4.

7.3.3 Preserved organic carbon

Globally, the carbon lost through respiration and decomposition approximately matches the carbon gained by plants through photosynthesis. The reservoir of carbon in plants does not greatly increase or decrease but, nevertheless, there is an imbalance in the carbon cycle today. This imbalance is evidenced by the increase in atmospheric CO_2 over the last 200 years, as shown in Figure 7.7, which plots the number of CO_2 molecules in every one million particles (atoms and molecules) in the atmosphere from about 1745 to the present day. This is a result of human activities because of the rapid release of carbon into the atmosphere from burning fossil fuels – carbon that was slowly captured from the ancient atmosphere by photosynthesis millions of years ago. The flow rate of carbon into the preserved organic carbon reservoir is very slow (Figure 7.6). However, post-industrialisation, humans have developed an appetite for burning fossil fuels that has no precedent, giving the much higher flow rate from the preserved organic carbon reservoir to the atmosphere. We shall return to this point in Section 7.4.

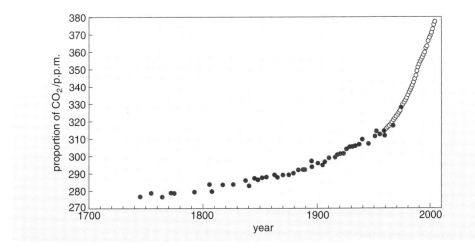

Figure 7.7 Proportion (in parts per million or p.p.m.) of CO_2 in the atmosphere over the past 250 years, as indicated by air trapped in Antarctic ice (filled circles) and by direct monitoring at Mauna Loa observatory (open circles).

● What do you notice about the rate of increase in atmospheric CO_2 shown in Figure 7.7?

◍ Not only has the proportion of CO_2 in the atmosphere been increasing since the mid-1700s but the rate of increase is also increasing. This is shown by the upward curve of the graph. A steady rate of increase would be a straight line.

7.3.4 Summary of the carbon cycle

As noted earlier, the carbon cycle is more complex than the water cycle because of the wide range of molecular forms that carbon can take, the many reservoirs involved, and the huge range of residence times. In discussing the four key reservoirs for exchanges of CO_2 with the atmosphere, we have neglected to highlight many other processes in the cycle, such as the small net absorption of atmospheric CO_2 directly into the oceans, the transport of soil and detritus into the ocean through runoff from land, and the slow return of carbon to the atmosphere from the ocean by the formation of carbonate rocks and their subsequent disintegration, among others. There is a more complete summary of the carbon cycle, giving the reservoir sizes, flow rates between reservoirs and some of the time-scales for the flows, in Figure 7.8, which you might like to study. The four key reservoirs that were described previously are in the left-hand side of the figure.

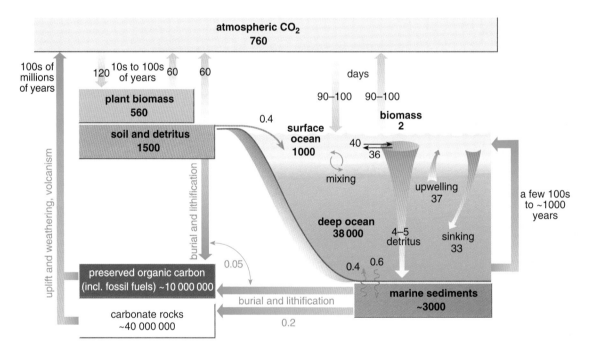

Figure 7.8 A more detailed summary of the global carbon cycle. The approximate mass of each reservoir is given in units of 10^{12} kg C. The flow rates between reservoirs (shown on the arrows) are given in units of 10^{12} kg C y^{-1}, and the time-scales for these flows are also indicated. Human contributions and current imbalances are not included.

7.4 The increasing concentration of carbon dioxide

It is clear from Figure 7.7 that there is a continuing and dramatic rise in the concentration of CO_2 in the atmosphere. However, long-term variation is not the only variation: there is also a very clear annual variation in CO_2, as shown in Figure 7.9.

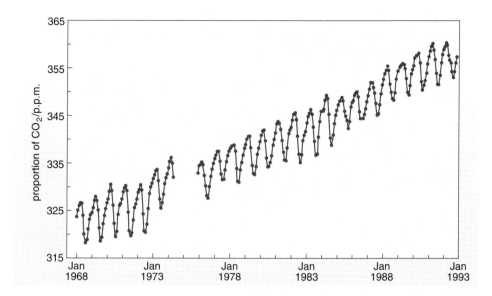

Figure 7.9 Month-by-month record of the proportion of CO_2 (in p.p.m.) in the atmosphere, as measured in Colorado, USA.

● From Figure 7.9, when is the highest CO_2 concentration each year – in the summer or the winter? What do you think might be causing this annual variation?

◉ The highest CO_2 level is in the winter, while the lowest is in summer. The annual variation is caused by a combination of factors. First, in the summer, vegetation is most actively growing, so photosynthesis, the process by which CO_2 is taken in by the plants (see Section 7.3.1), is at its most effective. Second, in the winter large quantities of fossil fuel are burned for heating and lighting, so large quantities of CO_2 are released, thus elevating the atmospheric concentrations.

A proxy (substitute) measure of the amount of photosynthesis is the greenness of vegetation as measured by satellite monitoring (Figure 7.10). The more

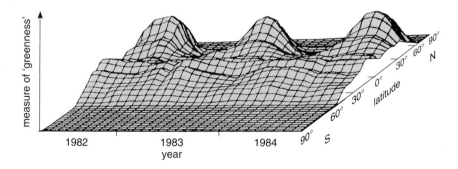

Figure 7.10 Annual variation in the amount of vegetation 'greenness'. The vertical axis gives the measure of greenness, which is plotted against time over three years, for a range of latitudes. The three most prominent 'bumps' show that the amount of greenness peaks between latitudes 30° N and 60° N in the middle of each year, i.e. during the Northern Hemisphere summer.

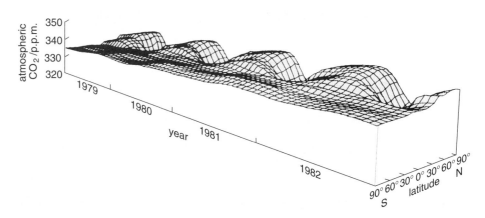

Figure 7.11 Annual variation in atmospheric CO_2 concentration. The vertical axis gives the atmospheric CO_2 concentration, which is plotted against time over four years, for a range of latitudes.

photosynthesis there is, the greener the plant cover. The effect of vegetation taking up atmospheric CO_2 is enough to cause a measurable fall in CO_2, which is shown against both time and latitude in Figure 7.11.

● By comparing Figures 7.10 and 7.11 and referring to Figure 1.4, why do you think the plots have these shapes in relation to latitude?

◉ Figure 1.4 shows that the amount of land supporting vegetation is much greater in the Northern Hemisphere than in the Southern Hemisphere. The north also supports a far bigger human population in highly industrialised societies and hence large-scale fuel use (in North America, Europe and Asia). Consequently, the annual fluctuation in CO_2 concentrations is much greater in the Northern Hemisphere.

If you look carefully at Figure 7.11 you will see shallow humps in the Southern Hemisphere in line with the pronounced troughs in the Northern Hemisphere. These represent the vegetation in South America, Australia, etc., which shows a maximum amount of photosynthesis in the southern summer, but this activity is small compared with that of the more extensive vegetation in the north.

● What does the shape of these graphs tell us about large-scale atmospheric circulation between the Northern and Southern Hemispheres?

◉ The strong Northern Hemisphere effects are largely restricted to the Northern Hemisphere and do not spill over into the Southern Hemisphere within the annual cycle. This suggests that the air masses in each hemisphere are more or less isolated from each other, at least on these time-scales.

You can see why this is the case by looking at the global circulation maps shown in Figure 6.5 (for the ocean world) and Figure 6.12 (for the real Earth). They show negligible flow across the Equator because air rises at the ITCZ and is returned to the hemisphere it came from. However, over a period of a few years, mixing between hemispheres does take place.

Figures 7.7, 7.9 and 7.11 show that the CO_2 concentration in the atmosphere is rising and at an accelerating rate. It is also increasing everywhere – this is a global trend. There are no known natural processes that could cause such a dramatic increase in atmospheric CO_2 over such a short time. However, the Industrial Revolution, which saw a huge increase in the use of coal as a source of energy, began in Europe during the 18th century. Economies all over the world have become more and more industrialised since then, consuming ever-increasing amounts of fossil fuel (oil and gas, as well as coal). This fossil-fuel carbon is now being released back into the atmosphere on a time-scale that is many orders of magnitude shorter than the time it took to be captured by photosynthesis and preserved. The consumption of fossil fuel also coincides with the observed increase in atmospheric CO_2 level. A second human influence is deforestation. One consequence of converting large areas of tropical rainforest into agricultural land is that less carbon is stored in biomass. When this wood is burned, as is usually the case, the carbon in the wood becomes CO_2 in the atmosphere. The rate of deforestation, especially in the tropics, has increased dramatically since the 1970s.

Thus, the amount of atmospheric CO_2 has increased along with the increased consumption of fossil fuels and clearance of tropical forests. Many people are convinced that this is far more than a coincidence.

The rate at which carbon was being added to the atmosphere by human activity in the 1990s is known to a reasonable degree of accuracy: a total of about 7×10^{12} kg C y^{-1}. Fossil-fuel burning accounts for 5.4×10^{12} kg C y^{-1} (a value known to a high degree of accuracy), and the clearing and burning of forests for the rest (a value not as accurately known, but thought to be in the range of $1–2 \times 10^{12}$ kg C y^{-1}). So, although fossil-fuel burning accounts for most of the measured CO_2 rise in the atmosphere, the contribution from deforestation is not insignificant.

The atmosphere is a relatively small reservoir of carbon (mostly CO_2) with direct links to all of the other reservoirs of the carbon cycle and, importantly, to the preserved organic carbon reservoir (Figure 7.8). Therefore, small changes in any of these reservoirs of carbon can have a large effect on the amount of CO_2 in the atmosphere. This in turn might affect climate, through the greenhouse effect. Climate, then, is intimately linked with the living organisms on Earth.

In Chapter 8, we shall finally bring together everything we have learned about the climate system and find out how computer models are used to predict weather and climate, and in particular to forecast what effect an increase in CO_2 concentration will have.

7.5 Summary of Chapter 7

1   The Earth's atmosphere is a mixture of different gases, primarily molecular nitrogen and oxygen.

2   The type and number of atoms in a molecule determine whether its gas absorbs infrared radiation or not. Molecular oxygen and nitrogen (the predominant gases in the Earth's atmosphere) do not absorb infrared radiation, whereas the two minor constituents (carbon dioxide and water vapour) do, and are therefore called greenhouse gases.

3   The Earth's surface temperature is determined partly by the amount of the greenhouse gases CO_2 and H_2O in the atmosphere. Without their infrared absorption the Earth's surface would be much cooler.

4   The amount of CO_2 in the atmosphere depends on the global carbon cycle. The carbon cycle is more complex than the water cycle, as carbon exists in different forms, for example as CO_2 in the atmosphere, as organic compounds in plants, and as fossil fuels. This means that changes in one of many different processes can lead to a change in the concentration of CO_2 in the atmosphere. There has been a significant increase in atmospheric CO_2 since the Industrial Revolution, which is believed to be a result of fossil-fuel burning.

8 Climate models

This chapter draws on the knowledge developed in Chapters 1 to 7, to see what we can say about the future evolution of the Earth's climate, and how certain we can be of the forecasts that climate models have produced. Previously, we have seen how the balance between heating and cooling of the Earth, its atmosphere and the oceans is affected by the amount of carbon dioxide (CO_2) and other greenhouse gases in the atmosphere. We have also seen how energy is moved from equatorial regions to polar regions by winds. Ocean currents, which we did not discuss here, are also important for energy transport. Together, these and the other effects we have considered produce changes in the global mean surface temperature (GMST). Historical records since pre-industrialisation times provide clear evidence of an increase in the CO_2 content and GMST over the last 100 years. What we now want to know is how the Earth's climate will change over the next 100 years.

First, we must introduce the models that are used in making these predictions before moving on to look at the predictions in more detail.

8.1 Building climate models

At the end of Chapter 1, we spoke about the simplest kind of climate model: energy balance models or EBMs. These can be very useful for doing simple experiments, such as finding out how much the Earth's temperature will change if we alter some of its surface or atmospheric characteristics, or indeed whether the amount of heat given out by the Sun changes, but this kind of model only gives us one value: the average temperature of the Earth. It does not tell us what the temperature will be at any given place on the Earth.

8.1.1 General circulation models (GCMs)

In fairly simple models, such as the energy balance models, scientists try to reduce the complex behaviour of the climate down to a set of mathematical equations, in the hope that they can then begin to understand the processes that are going on. However, with state-of-the-art general circulation models (GCMs), it is more a case of trying to represent everything, even if it then gets so complicated that we can't always understand what is happening. The equations are tweaked, within reasonable boundaries, so that the model does as well as possible at reproducing past and current climates (compared with archived observations). The model can then be used to try to predict what the climate will do in the future.

To produce a GCM, we make our energy balance model more complicated. Instead of using the whole of the Earth's surface as one, we can divide it up into smaller pieces. For example, we can divide it into bands parallel to latitude, and each of these bands can be divided into segments based on longitudinal divisions. If our divisions are small enough we will end up with our 1 m × 1 m plot from Section 1.4.

'Never trust a computer you can't throw out of the window.'
Steve Wozniac

135

To understand weather we need to know more than just the temperature of the whole of the Earth's surface; we need to know something about the measurable characteristics of the air. We can start this by, for example, dividing the air up into segments, just as we divided up the Earth's surface into segments in Section 1.4. Above our 1 m × 1 m area of soil we can add a 1 m thickness of air. Effectively we now have a 1 m × 1 m × 1 m block of air – a cubic metre. If we know how much that volume of air will heat up with a given amount of heat absorbed, some from the ground below it and some directly from the Sun above, we can start to get a basic measurable property of that part of the atmosphere – its temperature. Of course, now each block of air is also receiving heat and losing heat to its neighbouring blocks so the situation can start to get quite complicated. In reality the Earth's atmosphere is much thicker than 1 m, so we have to stack many blocks of air on top of one another to represent the thickness of the atmosphere.

By now you should appreciate that the complexity has only just begun. What is more, the way in which the air in each block absorbs and radiates heat is also slightly different, depending on how much water vapour there is in it, how many air molecules are in the block, how the radiation interacts with the molecules in the atmosphere (e.g. the way the air moves, clouds form and precipitation falls, ice-sheets grow or shrink), etc. As if that wasn't enough, the amount of heat each block receives from the Sun varies with the time of day, the seasons, whether clouds form above it, and so on. Moreover, air can move, so there is also a physical exchange of air between our blocks. In addition to having ground and atmospheric layers represented as described above, climate models are frequently coupled to a representation of the ocean and may also take into account how the vegetation on the Earth's surface changes. Critically, they try to calculate how all these different parts of the climate system interact, and how the feedback processes work.

This complex situation is the basis for the models used to forecast both weather and climate. The 'best' estimates of future climate come from GCMs, rather than simplified models such as EBMs.

8.1.2 Dividing up time and space

The sets of equations that comprise numerical models of weather are, by their very nature, highly complex. To reproduce all the motions of just part of the weather system – the atmosphere – we would have to reproduce the movement and interactions of every gas molecule. Clearly, this cannot be done. Simplifications have to be made, so most modern numerical models used to forecast weather and climate divide the atmosphere into blocks that are much larger than the 1 m × 1 m × 1 m cube we considered above, and reproduce what goes on within and between each block. The size of the blocks is determined by an imaginary grid laid out on the Earth's surface. Over each grid the atmosphere is divided into several layers, so you can think of the blocks as being a series of adjacent 'boxes' of air, whose sizes are determined by the spacing of the grid and the number of layers in the atmosphere.

In a similar way to the horizontal grid, the vertical resolution of a model is a compromise between accuracy and computer time. As we saw in Chapter 5, the Earth's atmosphere has a thickness of a few tens of kilometres, and becomes

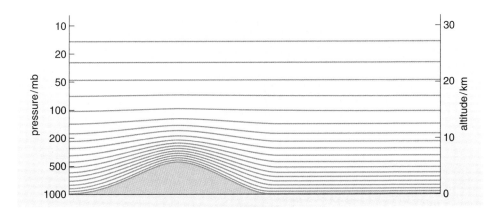

Figure 8.1 The model layers used by climate*prediction*.net and an example of how they are modified over a mountain. Note that the layers are not equally spaced in altitude (right-hand scale) or pressure (left-hand scale).

progressively less dense with increasing altitude. In the climate*prediction*.net model, for example, there are 19 levels in the atmosphere but they are not of equal thickness (see Figure 8.1). The layers nearest the ground must also take account of the shape of the ground surface and follow the contours of the land surface, so that the layer does not suddenly disappear into a mountainside!

● Figure 8.1 shows there are more layers at lower altitudes than higher in the atmosphere. Why do you think this is?

◉ This is because we are more interested in the processes that go on near the ground, where the dynamics of the atmosphere are more complex. The uppermost layer is at an altitude of about 30 km, where the density of the air is only 1% of that at sea-level.

Figure 8.2 shows how the vertical and horizontal resolutions together determine the size of the boxes in the climate model.

The passage of time is also divided up into steps. The length of a typical time-step in a climate model might be 30 minutes. A model starts from a set of initial conditions for the atmosphere and ocean and then calculates what they will have evolved to after 30 minutes, 1 hour, etc. The model calculates the incoming energy from the Sun, the amount absorbed and reflected and the temperature, the humidity and the air pressure (to name but a few variables) within each box of air. Not only that, all the interactions with the adjacent boxes to the sides, above and below are also being calculated. It usually takes several seconds of computer time to do all the calculations for each 30-minute step of model time. Choosing the time-step is not easy. If you want to run a model through 50 years as quickly as possible, you should use as large a time-step as possible.

Figure 8.2 The grid spacing used in the climate*prediction*.net model, shown for the British Isles. The land area is covered by three grids in the east–west direction and four in the north–south direction. Within each grid the atmosphere is divided into 19 layers. In this way, the atmosphere is divided into boxes. Note that the scale is exaggerated in the vertical direction: while each grid is about 250 km wide, the vertical stack of 19 levels extends to only 30 km.

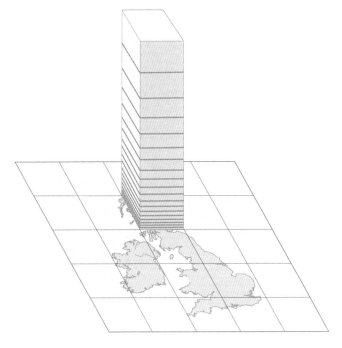

- Can you think why it is not possible to choose an arbitrarily large time-step?

- With a time-step bigger than some critical level, too many changes happen for the calculations to be reliable, and the model becomes unstable and stops working. In very simplified terms, you can think of this as happening when the time-step is so large that air or energy can travel further than one grid box in one time-step, and it becomes impossible to determine accurately how the variables change.

Some aspects of the atmosphere change more rapidly than others and so need to be calculated more frequently. For example, the dynamics (essentially the movement of the air) may need to be calculated every 30 minutes, but the radiation (the balance of incoming and outgoing energy) can be calculated less frequently.

The sizes of the atmospheric boxes and the duration of the time-steps determine the resolution of the model. The higher the resolution, the finer-scale the details of the Earth's surface (such as peninsulas and mountains) and atmosphere (such as clouds) that can be represented. High-resolution models with relatively small atmospheric boxes and short time-steps are used for weather forecasting, while models with large boxes and large time-steps are used for climate models. This is because the climate models have to simulate much longer periods of time. Operating them at the resolutions used for weather forecasting would require vast numbers of calculations and would be too expensive in computer time – it could easily take several years to produce a climate forecast! For a weather forecast, which is only interested in the next five days or so, the resolution can be much finer than for a climate forecast that is concerned with the next few hundred years. The resolution of a typical climate model is shown in Figure 8.3. Modellers of palaeoclimates, who are interested in what the climate was doing thousands of years ago, have to use even coarser resolution models. Unfortunately, changing the resolution of a model can introduce large uncertainties into the results.

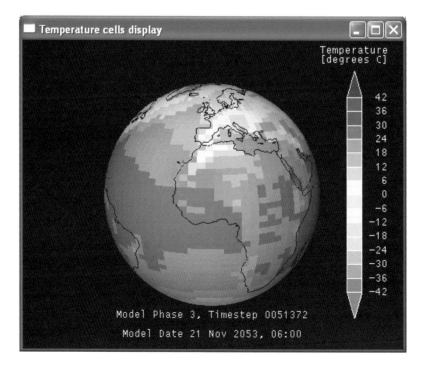

Figure 8.3 A typical display from a climate model, showing the temperature of the Earth's surface in each of the model grid boxes at one time-step.

Figure 8.4 Simulation of winter rainfall change (in mm per day) over the British Isles for two models: (a) a climate model with a resolution of 2.5° in latitude by 3.75° in longitude; (b) a model with a finer grid spacing that might be used to produce a weather forecast. The regional model in (b) gives a better simulation of British rainfall than the coarser resolution climate model in (a) does.

One example of a state-of-the-art climate model is the UK Met Office's Unified Model: the same model that is used to produce the weather forecasts on British terrestrial television. There are between 10 and 20 similar models worldwide. Figure 8.4 shows for the British Isles the difference in resolution between the model run to produce a weather forecast and the model run to produce a climate forecast. The resolution of the climate model is obviously of no use at all for telling people how much it will rain in Manchester (for example).

● What do you think the effect might be on what the model 'sees' of mountain ranges and seaways when a coarse grid is used as opposed to a fine grid?

● Much of the detail is lost with a coarse grid because it tends to smooth out high mountain ranges and close narrow seaways. This happens because these physical characteristics of the Earth's surface are averaged out over the whole grid square in which they occur. A narrow mountain range of, say, 2 km height occupying half the area of a grid square would appear to the model as a mountain range with double the width (i.e. the whole grid square) but only 1 km high. In many models, the effective height of the mountain range can be described to the model so that this effect is minimised.

To replicate the climate system fully, a model would have to simulate both the atmosphere and the oceans, which play an important part in the transport of heat around the Earth. However, this also adds large numbers of calculations to the model and means that it takes much longer to run. For this reason, many climate modelling experiments use a sophisticated atmosphere but a simplified ocean (a single layer or 'slab' ocean). This means that some aspects of the climate system (such as ocean currents) are not replicated, but the model runs much faster and many more calculations can be completed.

- Can you think of another example of accuracy being sacrificed for computational speed?

- The size of each grid box in the model is dictated in part by the need for speed. Smaller boxes would improve the sensitivity to local conditions, but would require very long computing times.

- Would the structure of a system such as Typhoon Lupit in Figure 6.10 be seen in a typical climate model?

- No, even at 1 300 km in diameter, the entire typhoon would occupy just a few grid boxes and these are not enough to reproduce the physics of such a system. Nevertheless, the heat transported from low to high latitudes by such systems is accounted for in the model.

8.1.3 Reliability and parameterisations

The reliability of weather-forecasting models is checked by comparing the predictions with the weather as it unfolds over hours, days and weeks. Observations of the weather are therefore needed both to make sure that the models are doing the right kind of thing – if a model can replicate the weather that actually happened, it must be reasonably accurate – and because, in order to make a forecast, you need to be able to tell the model the current weather, so that the model can be used to calculate how that weather will evolve.

The desired output from the models is an accurate forecast for every point over the Earth's surface. To achieve this, the mathematical equations can be tuned to match the observed weather. An example of this is involved in cloud formation – the model assumes that clouds are present when the relative humidity is above a certain value. The greater the relative humidity, the more cloud cover you would expect in the grid box. This value can be altered or 'tuned' so that the presence of clouds in the model matches observations of clouds as well as possible.

However, although the equations describe as accurately as possible the real physics of the atmosphere at the time-scale of minutes and spatial scales of kilometres, this tuning can introduce unforeseen problems when the scales are changed or when we try to investigate a climate system that differs from the one in which our present-day weather occurs. Modelling future (or past) climate is, by definition, asking the model to investigate a world that is different from the one we currently experience. A model that works well for today may not be so reliable for the past or the future.

The problem with dividing the atmosphere into numerous little boxes is that there are many processes that are smaller still than the boxes. So, for example, individual clouds could be smaller than a grid box. They still play an important role in the climate system, especially collectively, so somehow the processes that form them and the consequences of them existing must be represented. So, based on knowledge of the temperature and humidity in a box, we must estimate how much cloud and rain there is in the box. We also need to know how much dust and aerosols are in the box, as raindrops condense on to such small particles. The process of estimating these imperfectly known features of the model is called parameterising. There are many parameterisations in a model, such as a scheme which calculates how much cloud there is. Some of these schemes are well-constrained by observations and are believed to be quite reliable, but others are far less well understood and we are not very sure about them.

To show you what parameterisations are, Table 8.1 lists 20 that are investigated in the climate*prediction*.net experiment. Many of them relate to how clouds form and move in the atmosphere because these are some of the least understood aspects of atmospheric dynamics. Don't worry about the detail here. This table is meant to give you a feel for the kinds of parameterisations that are included in models.

Table 8.1 A list of the parameterisations investigated in the climate*prediction*.net experiment.

No.	Description
1	Ice fall speed through clouds – important for the development of clouds and precipitation.
2	A parameter which relates how quickly cloud droplets convert to rain.
3	'Critical relative humidity' – relates the humidity to the amount of cloud.
4	A parameter which relates how much water there is in a cloud to when it starts raining, which depends on the aerosol.
5	A parameter which determines how rapidly a convective cloud mixes in clear air.
6	Empirically adjusted cloud fraction – calculates how much cloud there will be when the air is saturated.
7	The initial state of the atmosphere when the model starts.
8	An effective radius for ice crystals in clouds – affects how much radiation is reflected, etc.
9	A parameter which allows for non-spherical ice particles in the radiation scheme.
10	A parameter governing how rapidly air mixes by turbulence close to the Earth.
11	A parameter governing how readily air masses mix.
12	A parameter governing the transfer of momentum and energy between tropical oceans and the air (wind) above them.
13	A parameter governing the transfer of momentum and energy between the seas and the air (wind) above them.
14	A parameter governing how water passes from the soil into the atmosphere by transpiration.
15	A parameter governing the diffusion of heat from the slab ocean to sea-ice.
16	A parameter governing the way air passing over a mountain loses energy as it oscillates up and down and gives out heat.
17	A set of parameters governing the way air interacts with surface features, such as mountains.
18	A set of parameters relating how the albedo of sea-ice varies with temperature.
19	The rate of mixing of heat from a warm air mass to a cold one by the random motion of particles.
20	The rate at which water vapour from a humid air mass mixes with a dry one by the random motion of particles.

8.2 The uncertainties in climate models

In Chapter 2 we introduced the notion of uncertainties in measurements. Climate models also have uncertainties, arising from the lack of perfect knowledge about the climate system. There are three main features associated with climate models which mean that it is impossible to produce a perfect forecast of the weather or the climate: the initial conditions the model is started from; the attributes which force the climate (Section 4.3.2); and the parameters which make up the actual model.

Initial conditions

'The flap of a butterfly's wings in Brazil can set off a tornado in Texas.' This famous quotation by Edward Lorenz sums up the fact that in some systems (the weather being one) very small differences in what is going on now can have huge effects on what happens in the future. As we cannot have perfect knowledge about what is going on now, we cannot make a definite forecast of the future.

Forcing

Some factors can have a huge effect on the climate, such as solar activity, the composition of the atmosphere and volcanoes. The particles and aerosols sent into the atmosphere by major volcanic eruptions decrease the amount of solar radiation reaching the ground but also help retain longwave radiation emitted by the Earth's surface. For example, after the volcano Mount Pinatubo erupted in 1991, it created a plume in the stratosphere which cooled the climate for several years. We call such factors forcing mechanisms because, when they change, they force the climate to change (see also Section 4.3.2).

Parameters

As we saw in Section 8.1.3, every climate model has to make many approximations, called parameterisations. Basically this means that there are numbers used in the model for which a range of other values could be equally realistic. By varying a poorly understood parameter in the model (see Table 8.1), a completely different forecast might be produced. It is also possible that some combinations of parameters may replicate the past climate equally well, but produce widely different forecasts for the future.

Whereas the initial conditions will affect what the *weather* is at any given time and place in the model, they do not have any bearing on the *climate*, which is purely determined by the parameters and forcing mechanisms. However, to be able to tell what the climate in a model actually is, you have to investigate the full range of possible initial conditions (or perform a very long model run with the forcing mechanisms held constant).

- Why is the location of the tropopause (Figure 5.5) in a climate model even more approximate (i.e. has greater uncertainty) than in the real atmosphere?

● In the model the atmosphere is divided into several layers and the thickness of these layers increases with height in the model atmosphere. The position of the tropopause in the model will, therefore, partly depend on the thickness of the atmospheric layers in that part of the model atmosphere.

Chapters 2 to 7 described much of the science underlying climate modelling but in this chapter you are now seeing some of the difficulties in trying to make detailed, accurate calculations of climate processes.

So, even the most complex models have uncertainties and these affect the results of the modelling calculations. This means that we cannot make definitive statements about how the Earth will respond to changes in the atmospheric concentrations of greenhouse gases. Nevertheless, we can determine how sensitive a climate forecast is to the uncertainties by making a large number of computations in which the uncertain parameterisations are varied over a range that covers the possibilities. This method, which is adopted in the climate*prediction*.net experiment, will reveal which of the uncertainties are the key ones and how the climate forecast depends on them. We shall now look at what recent climate modelling experiments can tell us about how the GMST, precipitation and other features of the climate may change.

8.3 Climate model results

8.3.1 Climate sensitivity

In Section 4.3.2, we mentioned how the size of the climate system's response to a forcing of given magnitude is called the climate's sensitivity. The sensitivity to CO_2 is sometimes defined more specifically as the difference between the GMST predicted by a model in which the atmospheric carbon dioxide levels have been fixed at pre-industrial levels and that from the same model when carbon dioxide levels are doubled (Figure 8.5). The climate sensitivity is therefore expressed in °C. It is a useful indicator of how a climate model behaves, although it is slightly artificial, of course, because carbon dioxide values in the atmosphere do not remain constant but change continuously (see Figure 7.11).

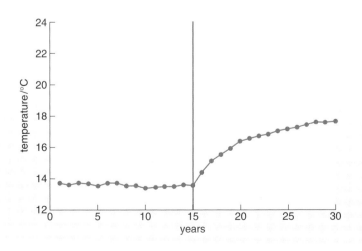

Figure 8.5 Change in GMST in a climate model with pre-industrial levels of atmospheric carbon dioxide (left of the vertical red line) and doubled carbon dioxide (right of the red line).

The first 2578 calculations of climate sensitivity that were obtained by the climate*prediction*.net experiment were published in the scientific journal *Nature* in January 2005. Each value of climate sensitivity was calculated by a model which had its own, unique set of parameter values and initial conditions. For comparison, the greatest number of calculations that had been completed before, using a supercomputer, was 128.

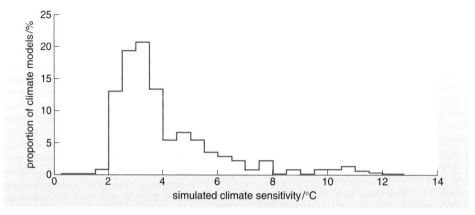

Figure 8.6 Climate sensitivities from the results of the climate*prediction*.net experiment in 2005. The vertical axis shows the percentage of climate models that simulated a particular climate sensitivity.

● From Figure 8.6, what range of climate sensitivities do most of the models simulate?

◌ The usual range is 2 to 4 °C but a few (5%), simulated a sensitivity of more than 8 °C, the highest sensitivity simulated being 12 °C and the lowest just under 2 °C.

8.3.2 How does climate sensitivity relate to the real world?

Climate sensitivity is a very artificial measure; it assumes that carbon dioxide levels are doubled and then remain constant for long enough for the climate to adjust.

In reality, greenhouse gas concentrations will change continuously in the future, but how? In 2001, the IPCC described 35 scenarios (possible alternative views of the future), each of which assumes a different pattern of economic, social and technological development around the world, and associated with it a particular pattern of growth or decline in global CO_2 emissions. Figure 8.7 shows four of the 35 scenarios that the IPCC considered. The projections of temperature change shown in Figure 1.7 come from some of them. These scenarios allow scientists to make some credible assumptions about the future, while acknowledging that the exact trends cannot be known yet. In addition to not knowing precisely how the concentrations of greenhouse gases may change, there are other uncertainties that may affect how the climate develops over the next 100 years. For example, we do not know how many large volcanic eruptions there will be.

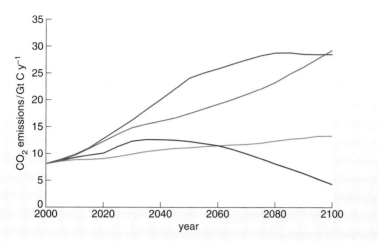

Figure 8.7 Carbon dioxide emission scenarios from the IPCC Report (2001). The four curves show four possible future trends in the annual CO_2 emissions in gigatonnes of carbon (10^{12} kg C) per year that have been used to assess possible climate change.

For the last IPCC Report (see Section 1.3), models with climate sensitivities between 1.7 and 2.4 °C were used to simulate climate change over the next 100 years, based on the 35 different greenhouse-gas emission scenarios. This approach was used because computer limitations meant full GCMs could not be run for all the possible emission scenarios for all of the next 100 years. In fact, the accepted range of climate sensitivity at the time of the report was 1.5 to 4.5 °C, a much smaller range than that inferred from the 2005 results shown in Figure 8.6. Using models computed for the 35 scenarios, and based on this small range of sensitivities, the GMST was projected to increase by 1.4 to 5.8 °C (Figure 8.8) over the period 1990 to 2100. This projected rate of warming is much larger than was observed during the 20th century and is probably without precedent during the last 10 000 years at least.

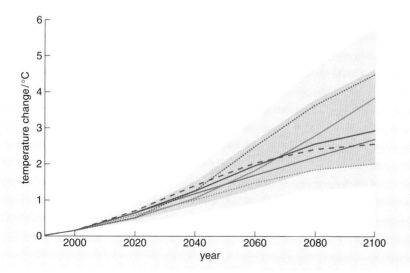

Figure 8.8 The projected change in GMST for six illustrative model scenarios (coloured lines). The darker shading represents the range of the full set of 35 IPCC scenarios where the mean climate sensitivity is 2.8 °C. The lighter shading is the range based on seven model projections with climate sensitivity in the range 1.7 to 4.2 °C.

Given that climate*prediction*.net has identified models with a climate sensitivity of up to 12 °C (Figure 8.6), it is reasonable to assume that the range of what the temperature might do in the next 100 years could be even wider – and will probably extend to even higher temperatures by 2100 and further into the future. The challenge is to find out what temperature change is most likely to happen.

8.3.3 How does precipitation change when temperature changes?

It is useful to be able to relate how much of a change in precipitation will be associated with a forecast change in temperature. Many things – flood defences, water supplies, agriculture, etc. – depend more on an accurate prediction of rainfall than on a prediction of temperature.

Models show that precipitation increases when atmospheric carbon dioxide is doubled (Figure 8.9). Why? You may recall from Section 5.3.1 that warm air can hold more water vapour before it becomes saturated than cold air. However, this does not determine how fast moisture circulates through the water cycle (see Chapter 5). This rate is controlled at a global level by how fast water can condense, rather than by how much water vapour there is in the atmosphere. As water vapour condenses to form clouds, it releases latent heat (see Section 4.1.2). If nothing removed this heat, the air would warm up and would be able to hold more moisture, so the condensation would stop. What actually happens is that the atmosphere gets rid of this heat, mostly in the form of longwave radiation (Sections 4.1.3 and 4.3.1). As the atmosphere warms up, longwave radiation increases (see Figure 8.10 and Chapter 4), which allows more cloud droplets to form, and so the whole water cycle intensifies.

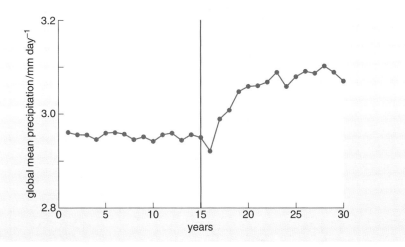

Figure 8.9 Global mean precipitation (mm per day) for a climate model with pre-industrial levels of atmospheric CO_2 (left of the red line) and doubled CO_2 (right of the red line). Note that if the CO_2 concentration is doubled instantaneously (as happens in year 15 in Figures 8.9 and 8.10), it takes six or more years for the atmosphere to adjust to the new steady state. The changes experienced in years 16 to 20 are transient effects that reflect the artificial way in which CO_2 is suddenly doubled in this model.

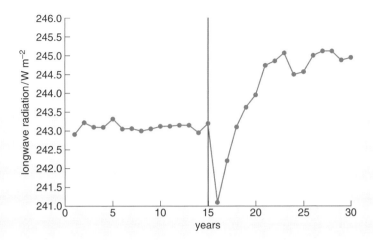

Figure 8.10 Globally averaged outgoing longwave radiation from a climate model. The point at which the amount of CO_2 in the atmosphere is doubled is shown by the red line. Years 16 to 20 show transient effects.

The extra rainfall is not equally spread around the Earth: some places get much more and some have a reduced amount of rainfall. Figure 8.11 shows the modelled difference in precipitation between an atmosphere with pre-industrial CO_2 levels and one with double that value. Changes in the distribution of precipitation can have profound consequences for human activity and wildlife.

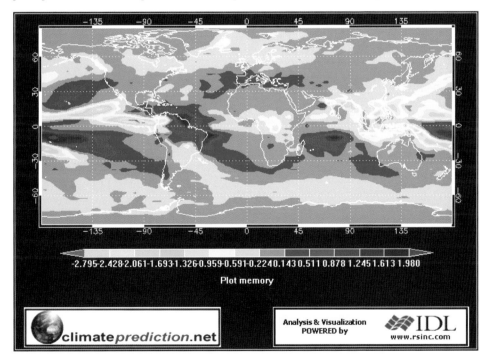

Figure 8.11 Difference in precipitation between a climate model with pre-industrial CO_2 levels and one with double that level of CO_2. A negative value indicates that the rainfall is greater in the model with doubled CO_2

- In Figure 8.11, where in the world does precipitation change most when CO_2 is doubled?

- The biggest increases in precipitation are in the tropics, associated with the ITCZ (Section 6.3.1). There is least change over Australia, Central Asia, the poles and parts of Africa.

8.4 Regional climate models (RCMs)

As you saw earlier in this chapter, limitations in the number of calculations a computer can do in a reasonable time limits the resolution that can be used for a GCM. Ultimately, however, the planners and policy makers who need to take a climate forecast and turn it into adequate water supplies, flood defences and food resources need information on a much finer scale. This can be achieved in several ways, two of which are described here.

'Downscaling' techniques involve using observations of today's climate to derive the relationship between large-scale climate variables (e.g. surface atmospheric pressure) and the climate at point locations (e.g. rain gauges). GCM predictions of the large-scale variables can then be used to predict the variations in the local climate. However, it may not be fair to assume that today's relationship between the large and the small scale will still be true in the future.

Alternatively, improvements in computing power mean that it is increasingly possible to use regional climate models (RCMs). These are higher resolution versions of GCMs covering a limited area of the globe. The calculations provided by a large-scale GCM can be used to drive the regional model and hence produce a forecast for the area of interest. The grid spacing of a regional model might be 50 km, roughly five times finer than in a GCM (cf. Figure 8.2). For this purpose, an RCM might cover western Europe or southern Africa – an area of about 5000 km by 5000 km. At its edges, the RCM is driven by the temperature, wind, etc. calculated by the coarse-resolution GCM.

Figure 8.12 shows the improvements in the prediction of precipitation over Britain when a regional model is used. Unfortunately, the computational costs of using an RCM are large and the results to date are limited to single simulations of a few regions.

- Why is a single simulation of limited use?

- This is because of the uncertainties in climate models and the uncertainties in the forcing mechanisms, such as greenhouse gas concentrations. Unless many computations are made for slightly different parameterisations, it is not clear how sensitive the simulations are to the uncertainties.

In the future, as computer speeds increase, it should be possible to use regional models much more extensively.

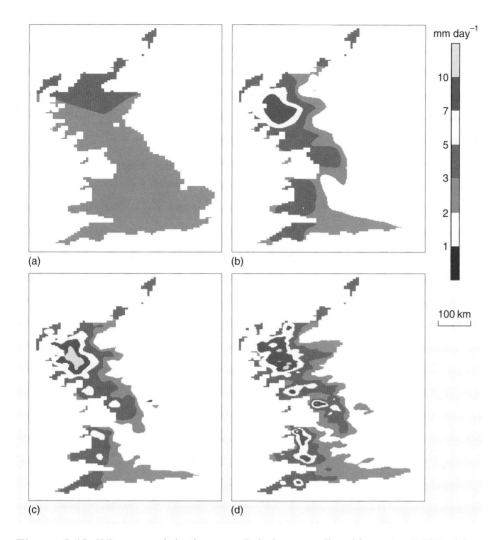

Figure 8.12 Winter precipitation over Britain as predicted by: (a) a GCM with 300 km resolution; (b) an RCM with 50 km resolution; and (c) an RCM with 25 km resolution; compared with (d) actual observations.

8.5 Summary of Chapter 8

1   Our attempts to predict the climate in the future depend on climate models. These are hindered by our lack of understanding of some important processes, such as how clouds form, as well as our incomplete knowledge of how the composition of the atmosphere will change in the future.

2   CO_2 values will continue to increase in the future. How much they increase depends on how the world develops socially, economically and technologically, and what legislation is put in place.

3 Climate sensitivity is defined as the change in GMST when CO_2 values are doubled. Current estimates, using state-of-the-art climate models, suggest that the climate sensitivity could be between 2 and 11 °C, most probably around 2 to 4 °C.

4 Simpler models can be used to relate climate sensitivity to how the GMST might change over the next 100 years. Changes in GMST in the range 1.4 to 5.8 °C are forecast for conservative sensitivity values, i.e. at the low end of the possible range.

5 Making a detailed forecast for a small region requires greater computer resources because it requires both a good forecast of the whole world and good information about the small-scale geography of the region.

8.6 Participating in the climate*prediction*.net experiment

If you have enjoyed this book and would like to try running a climate model on your home computer, you have several options, two of which are described below.

To download a model from www.climateprediction.net, go to that website and click on the 'join climate*prediction*.net' button and follow the instructions.

Alternatively, since the climate*prediction*.net experiment is continuously evolving, log on to www.climateprediction.net/science/strategy.php to see what the latest experiment is.

Ultimately, the climate*prediction*.net project will be able to use full GCMs to simulate the climate of the next 100 years and to use models which have demonstrated the full range of climate sensitivities.

Acknowledgements

Grateful acknowledgement is made to the following sources for permission to reproduce material in this book.

Figure 1.1: Associated Press; *Figure 1.2*: Reynold, R. (2000) *Phillip's Guide to Weather*, copyright © 2000 Phillip's; *Figure 1.5*: Frakes, L. A. (1979) *Climates throughout Geological Time*, Elsevier; *Figures 1.6, 1.7, 7.7, 8.7 and 8.8*: copyright © 2003 Intergovernmental Panel on Climate Change; *Figures 2.1, 3.12, 3.15, 4.5, 5.6, 5.12, 6.8, 8.1–8.3, 8.5, 8.6, 8.9–8.11*: climate*prediction*.net: *Figure 2.2*: © Crown Copyright, reproduced with the permission of the Controller of Her Majesty's Stationery Office; *Figure 2.6*: © European Centre for Medium-Range Weather Forecasts, ECMWF www.ecmwf.int; *Figures 2.8, 3.7, 3.9, 3.16, 5.1, 5.7, 5.9, 6.7 and 6.10*: NASA; *Figure 3.19*: J. Imbrie et al. (1984) in Berger, A. et al. (eds) *Milankovich and Climate*, Kluwer Academic; *Figure 3.22*: Rutherford Appleton Laboratory; *Figure 3.23a*: National Optical Astronomy Observatories/NSO, Sacramento Peak; *Figure 3.23b:* Lockheed Palo Alto Research Laboratory/ Japanese Institute of Space and Astronautical Science; *Figures 4.2 and 4.4a*: Bob Spicer; *Figure 4.10*: Van der Harr, T. and Suomi, V. (1971) *Journal of Atmospheric Science*, **28**, pp. 304–14, American Meteorological Society; *Figure 4.11*: Data courtesy of CERES instrument team, NASA; *Figure 5.8*: Image courtesy of the Total Ozone Mapping Spectrometer (TOMS) science team and the Scientific Visualisation Studio, NASA GSFC; *Figure 5.14*: Meteorological Office 1978, *Map of Average Annual Rainfall 1941–1970* (1978). Crown copyright material is reproduced under Class Licence Number C01W0000065 with the permission of the Controller of HMSO and the Queen's Printer for Scotland; *Figure 5.17*: *Water Resources: Planning for the future*, Anglian Water Authority; *Figure 6.2*: Burroughs, W. J. (1996) *Weather: the ultimate guide to the elements*, HarperCollins; *Figure 6.12*: Perry, A. H. and Walker, J. M. (1977) *The Ocean–Atmosphere System*, Addison-Wesley; *Figure 7.9*: Conway, T. J., Tans, P. P. and Waterman, L. S. (1994) 'Atmospheric CO_2 records from sites in the NOAA/CMDL air sampling network', pp. 41–119, in Boden, T. A., Kaiser, D. P., Sepanski, R. J. and Stoss, F. W. (eds) *Trends '93: A compendium of data on global change*, September 1994, ORNL/CDIAC-65, Carbon Dioxide Information Analysis Center, Oak Ridge National Laboratory, Oak Ridge, Tennessee, USA; *Figure 8.4*: Courtesy of the Hadley Centre; *Figure 8.12*: Adapted from Jones, R. G., Murphy, J. M. and Noguer, M. (1995) 'Simulation of climate change over Europe using a nested regional-climate model', *Quarterly Journal of The Royal Meteorological Society*, **121**. The Royal Meteorological Society.

Index